The Passionate Buddha

"Robert Sachs is himself a passionate Buddha,
as well as a longtime Buddhist practitioner, husband
and father, healer and teacher. I find a lot in this book
that helps us to further our sacred relationships by
learning to open the spiritual heart, deal with anger and
inner conflict, love and accept ourselves and others,
and live a more enlightened life.
Wisdom and love are the essence of spirit and
represent the innate qualities of awakened mind and
heart; practices of meditation and self-inquiry such as
those found here are the tools to unfold the marvelous
natural resources within us. I heartily
recommend *The Passionate Buddha* to all
on the spiritual path."

Surya Das, author of *Awakening the Buddha Within*
and founder of Dzogchen Foundation

The Passionate Buddha

Wisdom on Intimacy and Enduring Love

ROBERT SACHS

Inner Traditions
Rochester, Vermont

Inner Traditions
One Park Street
Rochester, Vermont 05767
www.InnerTraditions.com

Library of Congress Cataloging-in-Publication Data

Sachs, Robert.
    The passionate Buddha : wisdom on intimacy and enduring love / by Robert Sachs.
        p. cm.
    Includes bibliographical references and index.
    ISBN 0-89281-914-6
        1. Love—Religious aspects—Buddism. 2. Interpersonal relations—Religious aspects—Buddhism. 3. Buddhism—Social aspects. I. Title.

BQ4570,L6 S23 2002
294.3'5677—dc21

                             2002006076

Printed and bound in the United States at Lake Book Manufacturing, Inc.

10   9   8   7   6   5   4   3   2   1

Text design by Priscilla Baker
This book was typeset in Sabon with Quay Sans, Vivante, and Shelley Andante Script as the display typefaces

Dedication to a Friend

As we walked through the evening darkness up a mountain road near Santa Cruz, a good friend and fellow therapist engaged me in an earnest conversation about relationships in general, which led us to his own. A family and marital counselor himself, he was not ignorant of the pitfalls of and challenges to intimacy and long-term commitment. He heard about them day in and day out with his clients. But, more to the point, he was living them. A difficult marriage and bitter divorce followed by several unsatisfying encounters left him alone, lonely, and depressed.

He looked to me not only as a friend and therapist, but also because of my twenty-five-year relationship with the same woman—my wife, my partner, my love—Melanie. How did we do it? How are we still doing it?

And so, my friend, here is my offering—a testament to the value of Buddhist wisdom and practice in matters of the heart. I hope it is useful to you and to anyone we both ever encounter who cherishes affection and intimacy as a noble path to self-discovery, service, and joy.

Contents

Part One

The Foundation of Buddhist Ideals in Relationships

Creating the Relationships You Want

Sex and Sexual Matters

Introduction

*As human beings we have a basic nature in us
known as goodness . . . absolute goodness,
which is spotless, fantastic. . . . What is the
nature of that goodness? That goodness
possesses tremendous gentleness. Why is it
gentle? Because as human beings we can make
love. We can stroke somebody with a gentle
touch; we can kiss somebody with gentle
understanding. We can appreciate
somebody's beauty.*
—THE VENERABLE CHÖGYAM TRUNGPA RINPOCHE,
FROM A PUBLIC TALK AT THE UNIVERSITY OF COLORADO,
MARCH 12, 1978

TRUE LOVE

I wonder if it is a natural human impulse or notion to believe in
true love. If one reads works from some of the world's great
literary traditions, turns on a TV during the daytime soaps,
listens to anything from classical to rock music through the
ages, or even waits in a grocery checkout line, secretly glancing
at the tabloids or rows of romance novels awaiting a last-minute
purchase, this would seem to be the case. I know that in my
own life and in the lives of friends, colleagues, and clients with
whom I've had heart-to-heart moments, the very notion of true
love serves to define what is and is not valuable or acceptable
in a passionate, enduring relationship.

Personally, as naively idealistic as it may seem, I have grown
to have confidence in true love. I see it as the only path to

liberation and fulfillment for each and every human being. Yet for me to define what I or any other person really means by the concept of *true love* only evokes the Buddhist story of the blindfolded wise men who, each having touched a different part of a grown elephant, are asked to say what it was. Each one in turn hazards a different guess based on the specific characteristics of the area he touched and based on his own experience. Thus it is with true love. We have a sense of it based on our own life experiences. But none of those experiences adequately encompass the seemingly limitless facets of true love that lovers and seekers have felt, sung, and written about over the ages.

What then is it that makes a notion as seemingly indefinable as *true love* so enduring? Buddhist tradition teaches that our essential nature is basically good. This goodness, quite simply, is love. To be in love, to act in a loving way toward ourselves and others, is an external expression of how in touch we are with our own basic goodness—our own loving nature.

His Holiness the Dalai Lama speaks passionately about the value of human affection. Love, it would seem, is of primary importance. And, in the infinite way we as humans display love and affection, my sense is that all lovers and would-be lovers of the world would agree that romantic love is the most dizzying, confusing, challenging—and possibly the most endearing—expression of our loving nature. In a sense, in the bewildering experience of losing ourselves in true romantic love with another, we are actually finding ourselves. Not only do the two become one, but each one becomes more whole.

In the bewildering experience of losing ourselves in true romantic love with another, we are actually finding ourselves.

That said, I don't mean to simplify love as the answer. For the path we travel to fully actualize love in our lives is fraught with numerous pitfalls—almost all self-created.

To paraphrase Gampopa, the great Tibetan physician and Buddhist teacher, as he said in his work *The Supreme Path of Discipleship: The Precepts for the Gurus,* "It is the sign of a superior man that he treat all with equanimity yet still has a few good friends." Thus, Gampopa encourages us to identify with our absolute, unconditional loving nature while recognizing our personal preferences, our tendencies toward greater affinity with certain people. The Buddhist approach sees no real contradiction in this. Bliss and equanimity can coexist with personal happiness and satisfaction. Life lived to its fullest with complete awareness of what enlightenment is really all about can be full-bodied and juicy. Indeed, even the sacred and profane are not separate.

> *"It is the sign of a superior man that he treat all with equanimity yet still has a few good friends."*
>
> —GAMPOPA

What prevents us from embracing these paradoxes and this way of being is merely the force of habits reinforced over lifetimes, so deeply ingrained that they lead us to take our life circumstances and our personal characteristics far too seriously. The Buddhist approach to this dilemma and all the suffering it creates for us is to loosen these habit patterns so that we feel a bit more space. From this expansiveness we can turn around and gain a broader perspective; we can once again experience our loving nature. The practice of Buddhist meditation and techniques for self-transformation allows us to use skillful means and wisdom—expressions of the male and female principles respectively—in balanced action to infuse our real world situations with these ideals. What is the result of such an approach?

More than likely, in the tangled web we have created over our own lifetime as a result of our conditioned habit patterns, where we have good (perhaps more enlightened) and not so good days, the benefits of such a practice are ambiguous at best. Yet, over time we may notice in ourselves a softening, an opening, that allows more and more of the absolute view—which is an expression of our loving nature, our basic goodness—to shine through.

In relationship terms, we find it easier to have love and compassion for more and more others and, strangely, more likely than not, there just so happens to arise for us a special someone. If there is already a special someone, a Beloved, in our lives, our appreciation for who that person is—rather than how we want or expect him or her to be—grows.

The Passionate Buddha is about fully opening to our loving nature by breaking the habits we have created that prevent us from being in and finding love—learning to trust our heart, opening up to possibilities, working with our anger and other difficult emotions. We live in a time when divorce rates are high, unprotected sex can lead to disease or even death, single-parent families are the norm, cyber-sex is the dominant attraction on the information superhighway, and more and more people medicate their feelings of loneliness and despair. In these conditions, it seems imperative to offer a book that addresses how we can come to trust our loving nature, break the habits that alienate us from ourselves and others, and develop healthy, fulfilling, lasting relationships.

The "Wisdom on Intimacy" the book's subtitle refers to does not call for new learning or for cramming something external into our heads. Rather, it calls forth what we already know, deep down inside. Once we dissolve the tight grip of reinforced habit patterns that define how we see others and ourselves, a natural way of being emerges, one that is informed and inspired by our inherent and very wise loving nature. Our choice of action—even our choice of partner—is therefore no longer based on reflex or impulse, but on something more true to who we really are and in sync with what we really need. From a space of total noncontrivance, true love arises naturally with a mate whom we select and who selects us spontaneously and effortlessly—as if it were meant to be that way.

One of the premises of this book is that it is indeed that way and that there are practical steps one can take to make this happen. And any relationship—be it romantic, platonic, or other—that rests upon this loving, timeless, centerless center of being can endure almost any trial or tribulation. This is the secret behind creating lasting love. This is the Buddhist way.

WHO AM I TO BE WRITING THIS BOOK?

I have been a Buddhist practicing within the Tibetan tradition since 1975. And I have been married to the same person for almost the exact same amount of time. What I share here is the culmination of what I have learned (to date) from Buddhist practice that has guided my marriage, as well as what I have learned from my marriage that has enriched my practice of Buddhism. For it is my firm conviction that the heart of any tradition cannot survive unless its teachings are tested by and integrated into our everyday lives in a way that enriches the roles and relationships we develop as we grow; thus, its message comes alive with meaning rather than being sterile or dogmatic.

While I refer throughout this text to various Buddhist masters and their teachings, I want it to be clear from the start that I am a Buddhist practitioner and not a Buddhist "authority." I speak from my own life experience as a lover, husband, father, and social worker, who has spent uncounted hours listening to and being with friends and clients as they sought and worked on intimate relationships. All of these life roles have been influenced by the teachings and practices I have learned from honored Buddhist masters of today and yesterday. My intention in this volume is to offer what has worked for me thus far in the hope that it touches you, the reader, as well.

To illustrate my points in *The Passionate Buddha*, I present truths from the Mahayana tradition of Buddhism and share teachings of enlightened Buddhist masters of the past and present. In particular, I rely on particular poignant sayings from these masters that—in this age of relationship chaos and confusion—function as powerful tools. Through clever turns of phrase, these masters highlight what most of us go through in our relationships, and they remind us that it is possible to be different from the way we find ourselves being in the moment. In my twenty-five years of marriage thus far, I have found these bits of wisdom a great aid in breaking up icebergs and filling in chasms leading to potential disaster.

My commentary on these sayings is coupled with practical suggestions on how to integrate these principles in relationships. I also present meditations and visualizations that are useful for becoming more comfortable with ourselves and living with and loving others. Finally, I present a frank exploration of topics not frequently spoken of in Buddhist circles or teachings, but which are extremely relevant to all of us seeking or living in an intimate relationship; these include contraception, abortion, anger, wanderlust, and infidelity.

All in all, it is my intention to engage the reader as someone with whom I share the same wishes and dreams: to feel whole, alive, connected, and in love. That my insights come from my life experiences put within the context of Buddhist philosophy and practice in no way implies that the reader need be a Buddhist to derive value from this volume. For Buddhism is more a set of tools than it is an "-ism." Certainly there will be times when the Buddhist ethical or moral position on certain matters may seem to contradict some other religious views. Hopefully, for the discerning reader, this will provide food for thought rather than become a stumbling block. For the most part, however, the teachings and tools of the Buddha presented here are easily applied to whatever spiritual path or orientation the reader may follow.

In closing, I want to remind people that, unless we are God or the Buddha, life is a mystery. Absolute reality, our loving nature, can be approached only through the murky labyrinth of our everyday lives. You will have to take the teachings and sayings presented along with the anecdotes I provide and see how they fit in with your own life.

Expect uncertainty to be your friend and inspiration. Ambiguity rules the day. In fact, if you spend too much time trying to figure it all out, to get it all right, to be together and fully in control, chances are you'll end up miserable and alone. If you think you can figure someone else out or if you're living under the hallucination that you fully understand your partner or spouse, you are courting disaster for your relationship.

In the words of a wonderful female bard of the nineties, Sarah McLachlan, we are all just "fumbling towards ecstasy." Ultimately the path we tread or stumble along is our own, and we won't take anything or anyone else with us when we go. Yet although we are alone, we need not be lonely. If we open our eyes, relax our minds, and offer our hearts to those around us, there is no doubt in my mind that we shall receive in kind—and the journey will be that much richer and more joyful. Such a path invites intimacy into our lives. And with the experience of intimacy there arises a whole new understanding of what it means to be in a committed, enduring relationship.

Part One

The Foundation of Buddhist Ideals in Relationships

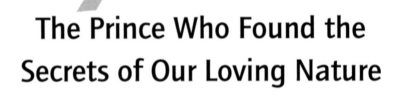

The Prince Who Found the Secrets of Our Loving Nature

Having enjoyed a delicious sweet taste,
And having sometimes tasted what is bitter,
Do not greedily enjoy the sweet taste,
Do not feel aversion toward the bitter.

When touched by pleasant contact, do not be
  enthralled,
Do not tremble when touched by pain.
Look evenly on both the pleasant and painful,
Not drawn or repelled by anything.
—THE BUDDHA (FROM *DAILY WISDOM: 365 BUDDHIST*
INSPIRATIONS, BY JOSH BARTOK, P. 62)

By the time Siddhartha Gautama was in his early twenties, he had it all. He was handsome, athletic, and brilliant. Standing in line to inherit a palace to put any mansion to shame, he was married to a devoted, beautiful wife, Yasodhara, and had numerous consorts and the finest entertainment to satisfy his every whim—day or night. A king-to-be, he'd even been blessed by his young wife with a strong, energetic son, Rahula, ensuring the continuation of his family's lineage and legacy.

What more could a guy ask for? Life seemed absolutely perfect—at least from a certain point of view. Indeed, most people would hold the view that it couldn't get much better than this.

But every point of view is just that—a small or perhaps even large dot in infinite space. Only those with limited capacity or those totally seduced by the phantasms of their own minds can accept any one perspective as the only game going. Thus, with his inquisitive mind and capacity for insight, Siddhartha could not completely embrace this illusion of perfection as being all there was to life. He sensed that there was more to it all.

And so, with a trusty, loyal attendant, Siddhartha decided to venture outside the grounds of his perfect royal domain—to go beyond the boundaries his parents had painstakingly laid out around him. He wanted to see what he had not yet seen and maybe scratch the itch he had not been able to ease in his palatial splendor.

Of course, when one goes looking for answers beyond one's usual borders, one rarely gets what one expects. And so it was for Siddhartha. Stepping into the world outside the hermetically sealed one he had been living in, he encountered scenes of life that taught him three truths he had never been faced with. He saw a sick person, an old person, and a dead person.

Siddhartha's parents had tried to shield him from the precarious and impermanent nature of life. Sick servants were always removed. Old ones were replaced with young ones. Death was never mentioned. For any pain or sickness the prince might have, there was always the finest doctor available to ease any malady that might suggest his own mortality. Yet, we are all aware of how our own bodies and minds change as we come into adulthood. Our very existence begs us to ask these questions: "What else is there?" "What happens next?" "What's the purpose in all this anyway?"

Witnessing possibilities he'd had inklings of but now saw to be real, Siddhartha was deeply moved. If all he had been surrounded by was as impermanent as all he now encountered, then the eternal youthfulness of his sheltered life was a mere contrivance and there was no purpose in perpetuating it for its own sake. After all, the people on the street outside of his palace didn't have such a luxury.

What was lasting and meaningful in living? Siddhartha was consumed by this question. His bubble of privilege—and with it his naivete—had burst. And late one night, under disguise, he ran off.

At first Siddhartha thought that he had to give everything up: his palace, his riches, his family and title, even his wife and beloved son. He joined the mendicant yogis in the jungles and beside the rivers. He starved himself, became a renunciate. For years he practiced many austerities. Finally, emaciated and near death, he came to the realization that he was no closer to answering his question about life by renouncing his humanity than he had been while languishing with angst in his palace of pleasure.

If having it all didn't work, and getting rid of it all didn't work either, what did work? At this point, Siddhartha came to his senses, took a bath in the river, and enjoyed a bowl of rice and curds given him by a girl from a nearby farm.

These were not mere events in Siddhartha's history. The acts of bathing and eating rice and curds offered by a farm girl had profound significance. For, according to the doctrine that Siddhartha, the Buddha-to-be, was to teach, wisdom is the activity of the feminine principle. And here the Buddha's story is resplendent with imagery that is wholly feminine: the water, the farm girl, the curds she offers. Gentleness and the simplicity of a young woman's common sense wisdom are what revived Siddhartha. Touched by the loving nature of another, he was able to reconnect with his own humanity and the preciousness of his own life. Thus, this event became an intrinsic part of his spiritual journey and the truth he was to share over the course of the rest of his life.

Refreshed by food and kindness, Siddhartha could see that neither the extremes of indulgence nor the denial of the senses was helpful to us as humans. There needed to be a balance. But to reach such a balance, to be able to avoid such extremes, was no small task. So, for six days, Siddhartha sat quietly. His years as an ascetic had given him great contemplative and meditative skills. These were now tempered with his new awareness of balance, so that he knew not to get all tight and twisted up; to relax, to experience gentleness and goodness.

Later on, the Buddha was to identify these two complementary forces in the process and full manifestation of enlightenment: skillful means, or the male principle, and wisdom, or the female principle. Skillful means and wisdom, the male and the female, are inseparable, both equally respected for the qualities they foster in us. For when the two come together, our actions are both sane and compassionate. We then act as a Buddha.

For six years, Siddhartha watched the gross and subtle ways in which his mind would vacillate between too tight and too loose, between too stoic and too sentimental. As he worked his way through his own psychophysical labyrinth to a state of perfect equanimity, all confusion was overcome; Siddhartha came to the balance and clarity he was looking for. Furthermore, he recognized that he was no different from anyone else, and that what he had found was none other than the inherent birthright of each and every being. What he had found and what he was now fully connected with was basic goodness—the loving nature that is who we are—resplendent with all the power and joy that comes with it.

In his translation of *The Tibetan Book of the Dead,* Robert Thurman, with poetic eloquence, portrays this liberation that Siddhartha and all Buddhas of the past, present, and future represent:

> Liberation—the cessation of self-addiction—results in a powerful and durable happiness, a vibrant and sustaining bliss. That special overflowing of joy makes the small worldly joys previously knowable in the tight trap of self-addiction seem paltry and pathetic. And the final bonus is that this relatively ultimate bliss, this supreme beatitude of the happiness of real freedom, naturally realizes that the lack of isolated, fixed, and independent self is just equivalent to the presence of all totally interrelated things and beings, inconceivably intertwining endlessly throughout

immeasurable eternity and unencompassable infinity. Free from all the cravings for nothing and oblivions, there is a personal destiny of endless involvement with limitless others. All this spurs you to share your happiness and to release the flow of your love, without the slightest diminution of your ultimate nirvana of indivisible bliss and freedom.[1]

What we see here in Thurman's breathtaking encapsulation of enlightenment, or of the experience of the enlightened, is a person who no longer feels isolated or alienated. A liberated, enlightened being feels totally connected with everyone else, and anything but the full and joyful expression of his or her loving nature no longer exists as a possibility; anything short of that full expression would be a limitation of the potential that being has now fully realized. In the words of Lama Ole Nydahl, Siddhartha now lived in the truth that "every atom vibrates with joy and is held together by love."

> *"Every atom vibrates with joy and is held together by love."*
>
> — LAMA OLE NYDAHL

Siddhartha—now the Buddha—could also see what it is in us that prevents us from experiencing this way of being. Each of us suffers in our own unique way, and that suffering is caused by what the Buddha called the Three Poisons of ignorance, attachment, and aggression. To translate this into our everyday experience: we don't have a full picture of what is going on (ignorance); we get stuck in the ways we see things and the ways we would like to see them (attachment); and we get mad as hell with anyone who disagrees with or challenges our version of what we think is going on (aggression).

Looking at these three, each of us—if we are at all honest about our experience—must confess to being poisoned. In our own blindness to the way things are, we build up biases and preferences that limit our reality and cut us off from appreciating one another wholeheartedly. Even our worst behavior as viewed from the wisdom eye of the Buddha is not rooted in our being bad or evil; we are merely misguided.

> *In our own blindness to the way things are, we build up biases and preferences that limit our reality and cut us off from appreciating one another wholeheartedly.*

It is interesting to note how modern psychology has labeled certain dysfunctional relationships as *toxic*—very much in keeping with the notion of the Three Poisons. However, where modern psychology asserts that this toxicity is rooted in our primary relationships in this lifetime, which need to be explored and worked through, the Buddha saw this as a personal, intimate issue for each and every one of us since beginningless time.* Lifetime after lifetime, individually and collectively, we have been influenced by these Three Poisons. They are always present in an unenlightened state. Dysfunction is the norm. Until we are free of these Three Poisons, our relationships will inevitably be tainted to some degree, hence dysfunctional.

Thus, the Buddha sought to introduce methods to transform the Three Poisons: where ignorance becomes an ineffable lightness of

---

*Beginningless time is a Buddhist concept that implies that there is no beginning point that does not have its own karmic traces as the cause. This cycle of karmic traces triggers habitual responses in endless succession and is represented in Tibetan Buddhist iconography as the Wheel of Life.

being and resourcefulness, attachment gives way to a vast and limit-less mind, and aggression is transmuted into sparks of spontaneity and joy. This he called the *dharma*.

In more parochial texts, *dharma* is translated as *the truth*, and sometimes *the path*. In fact, the term *dharma* embraces both of these notions. The more literal translation of *dharma* is *the way things are*. What is implied in this term is an understanding of how things are in this world and the methods one can use to transform the Three Poisons into qualities of enlightenment.

THE HUMAN PREDICAMENT: BUILT FOR PLEASURE

When the Buddha sat in his meditative equipoise beneath the Bodhi tree some 2,500 years ago, as his mind wrestled with the subtleties of too loose versus too tight, he was able to clearly perceive and identify Six Realms of Existence, each one inhabited by beings dominated by a particular negative emotional state. He saw that those dominated by the emotion of hate live in a state of mind and being that is hellish. These hell beings are so tormented, primarily by the experience of feeling overheated or frigid to an extreme degree, that they focus on nothing but their own suffering. Those dominated by avarice and desperation experience a ghostly existence. Whatever they want is almost always out of reach, and if they do chance to reach it, it never turns out to be the right thing anyway. Those whose ignorance leads them to be preoccupied with survival at all costs, and to pursue only what their biology dictates, live as animals always wary of predators. Driven by urges, they can never fully rest or feel at ease. Those who are jealous of what others have, wanting more than practicality may suggest or even more than is necessary for comfort, experience the negative emotional state of rich and powerful demigods or titans. Those who are intoxicated by the attributes and acquisitions they already have, who revel in illusion of the blissful perfection they are surrounded by, who are proud of their own stature and oblivious to the needs of others (unless those needs can somehow be manipulated to serve their own needs), are in the state of mind and being of worldly gods.

The five realms mentioned thus far of hell beings, ghosts, animals, titans, and worldly gods are not necessarily unique to the teachings of the Buddha. These types of beings exist in the mythologies and lore of virtually every culture in the world. The Buddha's particular offering was to clearly delineate the action of the Three Poisons in the mental state and actual being of the entities existing in each of these realms.

What, then, of humans? The human realm, according to the Buddha's teachings, is the sixth realm, the one he viewed as somewhat distinct from the other realms of existence. The negative emotional states that the Buddha saw associated with the other realms are relatively clear and their consequences seemingly obvious. But for humans, things are not so well defined. In our more ambiguous reality, the Buddha identified the predominant negative emotion or driving force as desire, or passion, which can lead us to get caught up in and preoccupied with the animalistic, instinctive side of our being, intoxicated with self-aggrandizement and our own self-importance. But that passion can also manifest as a sense that it is possible to connect with something more, something lasting and meaningful.

This longed-for *something* the Buddha called our Buddhanature— what he himself sensed, and what became the driving force in his own odyssey. This Buddhanature is the source of and is expressed by our inherent loving nature. Those who have a capacity to love, who can think of the needs of others, who are not so intoxicated by what they have or preoccupied with their own sense of need, impoverishment, or personal pain, are those who belong to the human family. We are passionate creatures in a realm the Buddha saw as offering the greatest capacity for choice.

In order to access and live up to the enormous potentials the Buddha saw as our birthright, we need not deny our passionate nature. Instead, we need to steer away from tendencies toward intoxication, like those of the titans and gods, and from the base preoccupations of the animals, ghosts, and hell beings; we need to open up to our Buddhanature and to its heart and expression, our loving nature. Passion is the core reason for our being human in the first place; it taps into, identifies with, and is transformed by our loving nature. It radiates warmth and joy.

Thus, for us as humans, the Buddha teaches a path that is directed to accessing our loving nature. Like all enlightened masters throughout time, he sees that in the final analysis, "All you need is love." More to the point, knowing how to truly love in every moment and every situation is the quintessential perfection of being human. Every visionary with this knowledge, who has also been graced with the desire and ability to teach, has developed his or her own methods and techniques to awaken this loving nature. In the case of the Buddha, what he offered as the foundational path to achieve this end is called the Middle Way.

> *Knowing how to truly love in every moment and every situation is the quintessential perfection of being human.*

In a nutshell, the Middle Way is a prescription on how to avoid extremes. It's a path for developing contemplative and meditative skills so that we always tap into and remain true to our loving nature; we learn how to manifest awareness of our loving nature in actions that are ecological and environmentally friendly and show honor and respect for each and every creature living under the sun and beyond. It is a blueprint for becoming a free, responsible, and civilized being in love with life in the fullest sense.

Of course, to achieve this is no small task. The Buddha could see that the Three Poisons, along with their variations of negative emotional states predominant in other realms, remain factors at play in each and every one of our lives.

Some, obsessed with or intoxicated by sensorial pleasure or the lack thereof—those caught up in the poison of attachment—need to be taught methods to lessen that attachment. They are prescribed more solitary or monastic lives, which include practices to still and uproot that attachment. This cooling-out process is designed to help such people reconnect to their loving nature and begin the process of being able to manifest it. This is the basis for what is now called the *Theravadin* or *Hinayana* (or Lesser Vehicle) school of Buddhism.

For those who have a more critical or aggressive nature but are not so caught up in their own needs or wants, who, therefore, already have or even exhibit the capacity to think of others, the Buddha taught the *Mahayana* (or Greater Vehicle) path. This is a path by which our loving nature is tapped into directly, and interactions are the test of how well we are in touch with and can express that nature. Here the Buddha speaks of *bodhicitta,* or Awakened Heart. He gives beings of this capacity methods to access, experience, and manifest pure love in their day-to-day lives. This pure love is not some metaphysical intangible, but rather experiential and interactive. In the case of a householder leading a life based on Mahayana principles, romantic love is clearly an acceptable, if not encouraged, manifestation.

As a distinct approach within Mahayana, the Buddha offered even more direct methods. To those whose love was overflowing, who could see in the Buddha what they themselves wanted to express in their own lives, he gave visualizations of archetypes, mantras (or sacred sounds), and other methods to engage each and every sense in the experience of full Awakened Heart. These are the Tantric methods of what is called the *Vajrayana*—the Diamond Vehicle.

Complete enlightenment, as so aptly described in the earlier-cited quote by Robert Thurman, is the fruition of perfecting the Mahayana and Vajrayana paths. The perfection or enlightenment that results from traveling the Hinayana path is foundational to this complete enlightenment. This does not mean, however, that the Hinayana is not as good as Mahayana or Vajrayana. As modern author and nun Pema Chödrön has emphasized in her work and writings, we need to start where we are. The path to enlightenment is an individual one. No one can walk in our shoes. Some of us may need to start the path on our own, but, in the end, it is with the help and in the presence of friends and others with whom we now share an exquisite intimacy that we arrive at our destination and reclaim our birthright.

As we fully access Awakened Heart and express our loving nature, we become what the Venerable Chögyam Trungpa Rinpoche called a "darling of the world." He has also referred to this as being the "ultimate warrior"—a warrior with a strong back and a soft front, with a fishhook piercing the sinews of the heart, the line being pulled constantly by the world around us. Bliss and the pain that comes with true, deep connection are inextricably linked as one—each defining the other. In remaining connected to our world and in touch with an exquisite clarity and bliss, we no longer fall prey to the illusion of separation, nor do we take personally the pains, trials, and tribulations that being in a human body, by definition, offers us. Through the pain of being, we remind ourselves of our origins. This, in turn, brings our "loftier spiritual experiences" into perspective, and we learn to express our loving nature in ways that truly make a difference to everyone we love and touch.

In the all too quoted words of Pierre Teilhard de Chardin, "We are not human beings having a spiritual experience, but spiritual beings having a human experience." It is through the full-bodied, red-blooded experience of being human that the spiritual beings that we are express love in a myriad of guises.

Because of their emphasis on intimacy and relationship in the fullest sense, the Buddha's Mahayana and Vajrayana teachings provide lessons, examples, and guidance that are quite well suited to helping us in the process of developing loving, lasting relationships—both generally, with all sentient beings, and specifically, with that special someone. This book draws upon the words of renowned teachers from these traditions.

Such insights as the great Zen master Sengstan's "the great way is not difficult for those who have no preferences" can help dissolve what can feel like irreconcilable differences of opinion on matters both trivial and critical.

Thus, Siddhartha Gautama, as the Buddha, shared his teachings for forty-five years. When he passed on (some would say he did not die), he felt that he had offered everything he possibly could to help us to understand that we are "spiritual beings having a human experience."

And what of his family and kingdom? The Buddha never returned to claim his throne or riches. But he did reunite with his wife and son. Because the accounts about enlightened beings tend to emphasize their miraculous nature and feats and overlook the mundane details of their lives, and because the cultures recording these accounts were male dominated, there are no nitty-gritty details of what Yasodhara and Rahula went through as a result of the Buddha's deserting them. Nor is there any account of what, if any, personal relationship may have been rekindled or continued between the Buddha, Yasodhara, and Rahula. What is said is that both wife and son were able to put down the burden of their personal history in the radiance and love that their previous husband and father, respectively, projected. But, still caught strongly in their attachments to the rich life, both took vows of monasticism: Yasodhara became a nun, and Rahula, a monk.

THAT WAS THEN. WHAT ABOUT NOW?

Because we are human beings and the Three Poisons of ignorance, attachment, and aggression remain evident at the core of all life's mischievous moments, our modern world and the one Siddhartha Gautama lived in are probably not all that different at a basic level. We need to remember that Siddhartha himself felt alienated from the world around him, and the path he took toward transforming his experience put him at odds with everything he had been raised to believe and everything he was expected to do personally, socially, and politically. He was willing to risk it all, to the point of deserting his family. Comfort was not a refuge; indeed, it had become a prison. He could no longer endure the isolation he felt from being disconnected from the greater organic world around him. No doubt, each of us—to a greater or lesser extent—knows what he was going through.

What is particular to our time, especially in the West, is that we have experienced a breakdown of cultural and societal barriers and norms that were, according to historians, more evident and operational in earlier times. In the Buddha's case, he lived during a time when the caste system of India was rigidly in place. For the most part, this theocratic culture defined what people did, where they lived, and whom it was proper for them to love or even interact with; the limits and possibilities in their lives were created for them. It was one thing for an untouchable, the lowest of the lowest, to seek the jungles and riverbanks and become a wandering mendicant or yogi. It was quite another thing altogether when a prince did the same.

A modern free market economy with democracy either in place or held as the ideal, in a world where there is a constant cross-fertilization of religions, philosophies, and ethnicities, creates a very different situation. No doubt we still see haves and have-nots, but there is a greater opportunity for individuals low on the socioeconomic scale to ascend to heights previously unimagined and for those of privilege to plummet to unthinkable depths.

In such an unstable and constantly changing climate, the definitions of the world around us that would hold us to one course—to a single shared cultural paradigm—are evidently tenuous at best. With the weakening or absence of cultural parameters, we are thrust out into a world where we have to find our own way. Unlike the Buddha, who had to sneak out to break free from the luxurious phantasm his family and society had created for him, we are placed outside the palace walls of the illusion of perfection—or any particular illusion—much sooner. In some ways, our dilemma is the opposite of the Buddha's: no one is creating a reality for us.

In the hodgepodge of the cultural soup we can mix and match concepts and notions to suit our whims. We can choose from an inordinate number of rules and norms from a variety of cultures that compete and conflict with one another. I think of this as the tyranny of excessive freedom. Our consciously and unconsciously adopted ideas might even be irrelevant to current conditions, yet they remain around our necks as yokes of outmoded beliefs or as collective human cellular memory that has yet to adapt to and integrate itself into what now faces us. As a result, even basic concepts as to what works in human interactions and relationships elude us. We are left bewildered and unclear as to what is and what is not useful or workable. As a species with tribal roots, faced with unprecedented choices in an overstimulating world, we are sorely tested to be able to handle such responsibility.

> *Each of us suffers in our own unique way, and that suffering is caused by the Three Poisons of ignorance, attachment, and aggression: we don't have a full picture of what is going on (ignorance); we get stuck in the ways we see things and the ways we would like to see them (attachment); and we get mad as hell with anyone who disagrees with or challenges our version of what we think is going on (aggression).*

This may be one of the primary causes of the lack of self-esteem so many Buddhist teachers from the East see in their Western students. Many have said that this is the opposite of what they face with students in the East. There, intact cultures and societal rules and restraints support well-defined ego structures that need to be tempered and softened by the Buddha's teachings on egolessness. Here, individuals are not given enough consistent cues to support a solid, independent self, and thus we vacillate, seeming wishy-washy and uncertain.

Many teachers find that they need to present the Buddha's teachings in a different way and style for the West. The Venerable Chögyam Trungpa Rinpoche commented that, in many ways, Buddhism fits into our culture more as a psychotherapeutic model than as a religion. As such, it makes sense that it has much to offer us, not only in the fields of depth psychology, but also in understanding interpersonal dynamics and relationships.

The so-called failure in modern intimate relationships has been expounded upon by social pundits and experts through every conceivable form of the media. The significance of this crisis has been noted by His Holiness the Dalai Lama, who, in an interview discussing such matters as relationships, families, and the great strife he sees in the modern world, brings his thoughts to a close with a rather provocative observation:

> If the parents are always fighting and finally divorce, I think that unconsciously, deep down, the child is badly influenced, imprinted. This is a tragedy. . . .
>
> *Happiness in the home will lead to happiness in the world* (italics mine).[2]

It seems that we are living in a Dark Age for relationships. Intimacy is on trial. Our loving nature, seeking to express itself through our humanity in this Realm of Desire, is individually and collectively being tested. In such a time of uncertainty, we are burdened with the reality of having to build relationships from the ground up. It is only this conscious kind of relationship that will be able to sustain itself in the chaos and related seduction of modernity. To build a modern, healthy relationship we need existential and transformational wisdom. It becomes a necessity to learn and develop the means by which we can know ourselves, discover our own personal habit patterns and tendencies, and come to terms with the assumptions we carry from our various cultural influences.

> *To build a modern, healthy relationship we need to learn to develop the means by which we can know ourselves, discover our own personal habit patterns and tendencies, and come to terms with the assumptions we carry from our various cultural influences.*

Placed in this context, the teachings of the Buddha become most appropriate. In a time when all sacred cows are on the slaughter block, each of us needs to develop the personal resourcefulness that is the foundation and purpose of the Buddha's teaching; we need to develop a sense of dharma—a sense of path and an understanding of how to walk upon that path. For the Buddha saw that in order for us to transcend the convention of society and its cultures, to truly become free, we need understanding and strength, wisdom and skillful means. With a discerning, independent mind we can learn what is the wheat and what is the chaff in what we see around us.

ENDURING LOVE: A BUDDHIST VISION

From contemplating the thoughts shared in this book and learning some of the practices offered, what can one expect? What does a conscious, loving, and enduring relationship look like?

The emphasis in Buddhism is on freedom, or enlightenment. Thus there are four key features that would be most prominent in a relationship based on Buddhist principles: flexibility, personable detachment, mutuality, and a growing universal love and compassion.

Flexibility refers to flexibility of the mind and spirit. Each partner works on letting go of habitual patterns and assumptions, meeting every one of life's circumstances with openness and possibility. Discord and disagreements are quickly transformed into an energy that is more playful and workable and can be used for new and more interesting ways of meeting life's challenges.

A *personable detachment* occurs as we transform passion into compassion. This has nothing to do with emotional distancing or killing passion in our relationship; rather, it involves not letting our desires or our projections distort or color any situation. When we open ourselves to a Buddhist approach to relationships we seek to become aware of our own biases, our own tendencies, and we learn to see them as our own and of our own making. As a result, we engage in fewer projections; we strive to no longer blame or praise our partner for how we feel, but see him or her as a catalyst in our lives. Our Beloved mirrors to us who we are, and we do the same for our Beloved. As a result each of us becomes a gift to the other and, in fact, the best of teachers.

Mutuality expresses itself when two partners respect each other as equals and cherish each other not only for who the other is, but also for the contribution each makes to the union. Operating from mutuality, we unconditionally support our partner's personal growth and defend the sacredness of the union as a catalyst for change for both individuals.

Finally, the love and affection we feel toward our partner and the specialness of our bond begin to expand into a *universal love and compassion* that has no bounds. As we learn more and more ways of opening up and sharing love and compassion within the couple, it is only a natural consequence that each and every relationship we have in the world becomes infected and infectious. Our love benefits all— which is the highest intention and goal in Buddhist practice.

There is a sixties song of the pop legend Donovan, who put into song a wonderful Zen saying:

> *First there is a mountain.*
> *Then there is no mountain.*
> *Then there is.*

These lines evoke that place where we all begin of having assumptions about the world, about ourselves, about the people around us. As we endeavor to cut through these assumptions through contemplation, prayer, meditation, and really learning from life's experiences, our assumptions begin to fall away, and we are presented with raw, new, exciting, sometimes even frightening possibilities. As we become more familiar with this state of openness, our assumptions are seen for what they are, the world becomes a bigger place, and we realize how much more is possible in our lives.

Lama Ole Nydahl shares this vision in almost every one of his meditations. In his words,

> We feel our own body condense out of space. It is power and joy. Something essential has happened. Before, we *were* our body and thus vulnerable to old age, sickness, death, and loss. Now we *have* our body. Body and speech are conscious tools for benefiting others.[3]

In today's world, if we are going to create a lasting relationship infused and fortified by the four features that mark an enduring love, we need to work with our minds and emotions consciously. No longer a victim of who we were or at least thought we were, we access our inherent loving nature and all the power and joy that is part and parcel of that nature. We embrace the world fully. We embrace all whom we touch. And even more exquisitely, we embrace our Beloved wholly and without hesitation.

From the outside, one might look at such a relationship and not see anything different from any other seemingly stable relationship. But in fact it is different. Buddhist principles encourage healthy relationships and healthy ways of being that ensure that each and every individual can learn, grow, and transform his or her experience at each step of the way throughout life. No doubt along the way there will be trials and tribulations. Such is the nature of conditioned existence, what Buddhists refer to as Samsara. However, in applying what the Buddha taught to our everyday life, each person individually and as part of a union will be equipped with a resourcefulness to meet such challenges with what in Buddhism are called the Four Immeasurables: great love, joy, compassion, and equanimity.

What follows are useful principles, contemplations, and tools from the teachings of the Buddha that will not only make you freer and happier in general, but also help you in breaking the habits that block you from intimacy and true love. The purpose in it all is to get you to think and open up—to help you to be able to receive and give to another *mindfully, sincerely, passionately*.

Meeting Yourself
with Meditation

*To love is first of all to accept yourself as you
actually are. "Knowing thyself" is the first
practice of love.*
—THICH NHAT HANH, TEACHINGS ON LOVE (P. 30)

In order to connect with and form an intimate relationship with
anyone else, we must have some sense of who we, ourselves,
are. And just as important, if not more, is our comfort level
with ourselves. For if we, ourselves, cannot accept what we
know of ourselves, how can we expect others to accept or feel
comfortable with us?

To have such knowledge and to demonstrate a genuine love
for and acceptance of ourselves is no small task. For we are not
speaking about becoming a narcissistic egomaniac celebrating
our own magnificence, but rather being a person manifesting a
solid connection with our loving nature, which allows us to be
with ourselves and others in a way that furthers an ever increasing experience of love unbounded. It is the kind of feeling
that we experience spontaneously around someone who has
done much authentic and heartfelt spiritual work—such as His
Holiness the Dalai Lama or Mother Teresa. No doubt there are

less famous examples that each of us comes across in our everyday lives.

Of course, being from the Realm of Desire as we are, we develop attractions to others whether or not we have much insight or real acceptance of who we are. At the same time, our connection and identification with our essence, our loving nature, whether it be conscious or not, is always in the background, informing our attractions, passions, and affections. The degree to which we have insight and acceptance of the truth of our loving nature shines through and reflects itself in the ways we are at times clear and open, at other times confused and awkward. We may "psych ourselves out" and back down from our hunches, not trusting our heartfelt feelings. Or we may find something inside ourselves that encourages us to reach through the fog, giving us what may seem to be a completely unwarranted confidence that all will work out—somehow.

In the long run, if a relationship that we forge with another is going to be dynamic and fulfilling, our connection to our loving nature will need to develop and grow. As life's lessons get added to the mix of our original attractions, passions, and affections, testing us along the way, we must go deeper into knowing our true essence.

It is for this reason that meditation is an indispensable tool, not only to progress in our own spiritual awakening—which inevitably connects us at a deeper level with others—but to actively further and ensure a greater intimacy with those we love.

> *As life's lessons get added to the mix of our original attractions, passions, and affections, testing us along the way, we must go deeper into knowing our true essence.*

Cultivating a close, warm-hearted feeling for others automatically puts the mind at ease. It is the ultimate source of success in life.
—HIS HOLINESS THE DALAI LAMA, *THE DALAI LAMA'S BOOK OF DAILY MEDITATIONS* (P. 105)

The philosophical and moral precepts that form what may be identified as the "religious" component of what the Buddha taught are not that different from those of other wisdom traditions. All speak of overcoming or transforming our hatred, greed, stupidity, desires, envy, and self-centered pride in order to express our humanity and the inherent love that is inseparable from and none other than our human nature. Each of these traditions, by and large, relies on contemplation and reflection, prayer, meditation, and altruistic activity as methods to accomplish the desired changes. In Buddhism, meditations are the primary methods for transforming these negative emotional states in a truly lasting way.

Meditation seems like such a solitary, lonely, maybe even daunting or frightening pursuit. How can such a practice affect relationships?

The Buddha saw that if we sit quiet and relaxed and free ourselves from being too tight or too loose (too intense or too spaced out), our loving nature will become more and more evident. As we become accustomed to just being—here and now—our identification with our turmoil and confusion is disrupted, and we can see them just as clouds coming and going in a vast sunlit sky. In the process of doing such a practice, we see how easy it is to get sidetracked, lured by one emotion or another. Thus, our compassion for others grows naturally as we come to understand how easy it is for others, too, to be trapped in situations that they may not even want but don't know how to get out of. With this recognition arises the altruism to be with and help others.

> *As we become accustomed to just being—here and now—our identification with our turmoil and confusion is disrupted, and we can see them just as clouds coming and going in a vast sunlit sky.*

As for connecting intimately with a special someone, the illusion of separation we've lived with becomes a thin disguise. We learn instead to trust the heartfelt warmth we see in their eyes and gestures, to recognize it as the same loving nature we are finding in ourselves. And, more than likely, this is reciprocated.

There are a multitude of meditative methods that the Buddha taught. Some rely on nothing but the breath. Some involve visualization or gazing upon an object. Others use archetypal sounds such as mantras to invoke specific qualities in our being. Still others have a particular philosophical or moral focus, designed, for example, to generate a compassionate attitude or to dispel negativity between people or in the world in general.

Although the type of meditation most suitable for each person varies according to his or her natural inclinations, the goal for everyone is pretty much the same. Success in meditation is evident when the person meditating becomes more open, flexible in being, spontaneous, and joyful—indeed, quite attractive in all that that implies. A countenance of distraction or gloom can make the prettiest of faces unattractive, while a joyful, vibrant way of being can make the most ordinary features seem radiant and magnetizing. On the other hand, overly serious or aloof detachment and stiffness in being are not signs of being spiritually elevated. Teachers manifesting such a character should be avoided. The same goes for lovers—unless you see a diamond in the rough and are willing to roll up your sleeves and chisel it free.

> *Success in meditation is evident when the person meditating becomes more open, flexible in being, spontaneous, and joyful.*

CREATING A REGULAR MEDITATION PRACTICE

Whenever we begin a new discipline, other parts of our life get shoved around. For most of us in the West, time is defined as schedule, and our schedule is more than likely too full to begin with. Thus, adding another thing to the list creates a new burden. This is the wrong way to approach meditation.

Imagine that you have been working hard all day. You walk into your house, take off your shoes, and just settle down with a nice, deep, relaxed sigh. Or, you come in from walking on a hot, dry afternoon, you pour yourself a long, cool glass of water, and you savor that moment when the cool wetness begins to soothe the parched tissues of your throat. This is how you should feel about sitting down to meditate. Enjoy it! Thinking of it in this way, it becomes more appealing than if you view it as some stiff spiritual discipline that is necessary to your self-actualization process.

This doesn't mean that you don't take your practice seriously. More than likely, in the beginning, there will be some amount of awkwardness in rearranging your life to fit it in, and a little serious push is necessary. However, like the Buddha who learned that too tight is as problematic as too loose, beware of developing an overly zealous or self-righteous attitude about meditating.

In the end, what counts is your sense of commitment to the process. Once you have embarked on your practice and you see what meditation contributes to your sense of well-being, openness, and flexibility with yourself and those you touch, it becomes easier and easier to continue in a mindful, joyous way.

> *Once you see what meditation contributes to your sense of well-being, openness, and flexibility with yourself and those you touch, it becomes easier and easier to continue in a mindful, joyous way.*

It is said that the final stage in the enlightenment process is that of No Meditation. Here, the mind is always in that state of tranquil, vibrant awareness. When we are no longer separate from that state, formal meditation as we know it is of little consequence. This may seem a far distant possibility. However, every moment of mindfulness brings us that much closer.

The four methods shared here—Calm Abiding, Tong Len Meditation, "Don't Know" Mind, and Passionate Visualization—are basic Buddhist meditation techniques that are suitable for men and women of any religious or spiritual persuasion. They can be used by themselves or as a foundation upon which other forms of prayer or meditation can be added.

CLARIFYING INTENTIONS

Before getting into the techniques, however, the matter of intentions needs to be addressed. For, according to Buddhist tradition, attitude and intention are critical components in applying meditation effectively. Buddhist practice hinges upon developing a greater openness and an altruistic outlook, and there are Four Thoughts that are considered foundational to this process. These Four Thoughts are presented here in a manner that reflects the intent to develop self-acceptance and open ourselves up to greater levels of intimacy in relationship.

Sitting down to meditate, consider each of these Four Thoughts for a few moments.

One: We appreciate the preciousness of our own life. The fact that we have the time, space, opportunity, and inclination to meditate in order to open ourselves up and to connect with others is precious in itself. Our appreciation for this gift deepens as we look around us in a world where people suffer from hunger, cold, disease, and various forms of persecution and repression.

Two: Recognizing the preciousness of our own life, we can also see its impermanence. Change is always happening. The present fades into the past. What we value and enjoy in our lives will pass, as will our pain and challenges. We cannot rely on things in the future being the way they are now. And, inevitably, we will die. Knowing the truth of this, we commit ourselves to treasuring each and every moment for what it offers us and we endeavor to use the time we have wisely and joyfully.

Three: What comes to us and what we experience, like it or not, is the direct result of seeds we have planted in the past—even though we may not see any direct connection. As we deepen our understanding of the way things are, the knowledge of this truth will become more profound. Appreciating the opportunity this gives us to become the master of our own future, to get the most out of the preciousness of our life, we commit ourselves to a path of opening to our loving nature with honesty and integrity.

Four: A life committed to self-preoccupation and self-indulgence will more than likely take us down many a dead end and leave us feeling lonely and disconnected. Not wanting to waste our time, and longing to heal any sense of separation from the world and from those who share it with us, we commit ourselves even more deeply to a path that honors our inherent loving nature and the human desire to love.

CALM ABIDING—QUIETNESS LEADS TO WHOLENESS

The purpose of the Calm Abiding (in Sanskrit, *shamatha,* and in Tibetan, *shinay)* meditation is for us to settle into a space where we have a calm and clear mind. It is an excellent method for developing equanimity—toward others as well as ourselves. Calm Abiding allows the agitation in our minds to settle, like silt or mud in disturbed waters. As the silt and mud filter down, the water becomes pure. A sense of wholesome aliveness arises naturally.

In this meditation we focus on the breath. Unlike breathing exercises in which we regulate the flow in and out, here we just observe the natural rhythm of the breath, in and out. This breath is what keeps us alive from moment to moment.

Step One: Sit in a comfortable manner. If you're on a chair, sit with your back away from the back of the chair so that your chest can expand fully. If you're sitting cross-legged on the ground, be sure that your knees are below the level of your navel. You may need to sit on a few cushions to achieve this. Generally speaking, it is best for your behind to be somewhere between four to six inches off the ground. If you know various yogic or meditative sitting poses, feel free to choose one of those. Allow your hands to rest, palms down, on or just above your knees.

Step Two: Allow your neck to relax so that your head is neither tilted too far forward nor cocked back. This means that your chin will be slightly tucked and your throat relaxed. Moisten your lips with your tongue and then rest your tongue just behind your top teeth on the roof of your mouth. If you're on the ground, your eyes should have a slight downward gaze, resting somewhere between eighteen inches and two feet in front of you. If you're sitting on a chair, aim your gaze between your knees, letting it go a bit farther. Your eyes are slightly open—this will help you stay grounded and relaxed. You are just sitting quietly in a room.

Step Three: Take a deep breath in and then draw up your pelvic muscles, tense your buttocks and abdomen, and straighten your arms so that your palms are pushing down on your knees. Hold this tension for a moment; then slowly exhale so that all the tension leaves with the breath and your sitting bones settle even deeper on your cushion or chair. Your diaphragm becomes soft and your breath now naturally rises and sinks from deep within you.

Step Four: Focus your attention on your breathing at the tip of your nostrils. As you breathe in, feel the air passing in through the nostrils and moving down through your abdomen to a point about one-and-a-half inches below your navel. As you breathe out, the abdomen contracts slightly and you feel the air passing out of the nostrils. Its invisible stream travels along the pathway of your gaze. As your eyes softly remain fixed on a given point, imagine that the stream of air dissolves about an inch above that point.

Step Five: You now need to become familiar with being able to stay concentrated on the breath. As you inhale, be aware of the breath passing in through your nostrils, but pay particular attention as the breath leaves at the nostrils when you exhale. As the breath goes out, count to yourself, "One." The next breath comes in, and as it passes out at the nostrils, you count, "Two." Continue to count like this up to twenty-one. If you get distracted, find your mind drifting from the counting, start at one again until you can successfully get to twenty-one.

This is easier than it seems, so be patient. Even after you become more proficient in meditation, you may find that counting to twenty-one takes more than a few tries.

Step Six: After you successfully count to twenty-one, allow your concentration to relax and just focus on the passage of air as it leaves your nostrils and dissolves into space. If you get distracted, just tell yourself, "Thinking," and then come back to the breath.

As an alternative to steps five and six, Lama Ole Nydahl recommends that as you breathe in, you imagine that the air flowing in is a translucent clear-white stream. As it passes through your throat and makes its way toward the point below your navel, imagine that the stream becomes red. As you exhale, the stream turns a deep blue color as it moves up from your navel center through your body. As it leaves your nostrils it is once again translucent white.[1]

Allow yourself at least ten minutes to start with, gradually increasing the time to twenty minutes. You can even extend this meditation to forty-five minutes to an hour. The important thing is to be consistent. It is better to do this meditation briefly every day than to wait for the weekend to do hours.

This meditation is also very powerful when done sitting next to a partner or several others. Such a sharing of calm and peace creates a sacred, trusting bond.

A Step Further—Sharing the Calm to Heal Relationships

Not only does this meditation create a greater sense of sharing when done with others, it also yields the same result if you simply visualize someone there! Let's say that your partner or a close friend is not around or isn't interested in meditation, but you want to connect with him or her in this way. Or perhaps you've had a difficult time lately with a certain person. This meditation can be a tool to heal or strengthen any relationship.

We are each a blend of male and female energies that are reflected in our psyche, our body and emotions, and the electromagnetic field or aura that surrounds us. Since the left side is female and the right side, male, imagine female friends, partners, or family members sitting on your left and place males on your right. Thus, you can evoke their presence in your meditation in a way that benefits not only you, but them as well.

This technique is as simple as it sounds. Just start by adding to your intentions what you intend to create with the person you are inviting into the meditation. As you follow the steps listed above, imagine that your partner or friend is doing the same—that he or she is with you here and now, participating in your meditation.

In the days or weeks that follow, examine for yourself how inviting someone into your meditation has affected both you and the other. Especially in difficult times, this meditation can create a new kind of openness that invites new possibilities when you're in the other person's actual presence.

TONG LEN MEDITATION—THE PRACTICE OF TAKING AND SENDING

In the practice of the Mahayana and Vajrayana paths of Buddhism, once we have come to the realization that nothing lives in isolation, that we are inseparable from everyone and everything around us, and that this at-oneness is also quite intangible and ever changing, expressing our loving nature fully and without reserve becomes effortless. As we are identified with and swimming in a vast ocean of love, our every thought and action is love manifest. What else is there to do?

> *Once we have come to the realization that we are inseparable from everyone and everything around us, expressing our loving nature fully and without reserve becomes effortless.*

This is the ultimate realization, what is known as ultimate bodhicitta. The end and test of Buddhist practice is to manifest this realization in thought, word, and deed in the day-to-day world. This is known as relative bodhicitta. In the practice of relative bodhicitta, our world becomes an automatic feedback system, providing us with an account of whether or not our thoughts, words, and deeds are, indeed, coming from this realization.

Because the essence of who we are is our loving nature, regardless of whether we do Buddhist practice or not, there are moments each of us has when there is an effortless flow between the ideal and the real; these are truly magical moments. And, more than likely, whether we do Buddhist practice or not, we sometimes make attempts to do what seems right at the time and find ourselves and the situation a bit more confused than when we started. It is said that the road to hell is paved with good intentions. This saying is meant as a strong admonishment to would-be do-gooders. However, if we are more charitable, we see that there are times we simply lack the knowledge or skill to put into action our noble intents. Thus, rather than question or show disdain for such intentions, we should strive to become more sensitive to limits, both our own and those of any given situation. We should, as the safety teachers used to teach us in school, "Stop, look, and listen."

One of the formal Buddhist practices that exemplifies our attempts to see a meeting between the ultimate and relative levels of bodhicitta is Tong Len, the practice of Taking and Sending.

Taking and Sending is the meditation that forms the practice component or the activity in *The Seven Points of Mind Training*. This treatise from the twelfth century, written by Chekawa Yeshe Dorje, was inspired by the original teachings of the great master Atisha from the eleventh century. It was most recently put into eloquent and earthy terms by the Venerable Jamgon Kongtrul Rinpoche in *The Great Path of Awakening*, the primary source for what is presented here. In addition to the material I present, I recommend *The Great Path of Awakening* to those who want to pursue this meditation as a serious component in their spiritual life.

In the context of relationship and intimacy, there are some basic foundational benefits to learning and practicing Tong Len. For one thing, it helps us to own our own projections. Atisha teaches that the first person we need to do Taking and Sending for is ourselves. There are many levels of meaning in what he is saying. At the simplest level, we realize that all of our suffering arises from our own unmitigated Three Poisons; it is therefore useful for us to breathe in and take back from the world around us the thoughts, words, and actions we've committed based on ignorance, attachment, and aggression. In that way, we no longer pollute our world and the people we love. As we breathe out, we send a breath of fresh air into the world; we create more space for others in our lives to be who they are without our expectations. As we own our own stuff and create more space for others, we become sensitive to their stuff, their poisons. We become more sensitive to why they are the way they are. As we breathe in, we then feel more compassion to take in and transform their pain and confusion and send out to them waves of love. As such, Tong Len is indispensable for developing intimacy.

What is offered below is a basic Tong Len meditation that can be done both formally, as when sitting in meditation, and informally, when dealing with difficult or painful circumstances on the spot.

Step One: Begin by sitting and adjusting your posture and breathing as you did in the first four steps of the Calm Abiding meditation (see pages 36–37). You come to the point where all you are doing is watching the passage of air at the tip of your nose.

Step Two: Begin the Taking and Sending with yourself. In your mind, make a commitment that as you breathe in you absorb all of your tendencies to project ignorance, attachment, and aggression out into the world. If you're stuck at this time with any particular negative emotion, you breathe it in, knowing that this emotion will color and distort your actions. The negativity that you breathe in goes to your heart, in which there rests a blue syllable, HUNG, written in Tibetan as ༄. Actually imagine this character or the letters H-U-N-G, or picture your heart filled with a deep blue light. This deep blue light is not only a healing light, but it is the nature of your mind. Allow the negativity that you breathe in to dissolve in the deep blue light in your heart. As you breathe out, imagine that pure, radiant love pours from your heart center and floods your entire being, then expands into the space around you. Feel this radiant love as clear and white, extending out as far as you can imagine.

Step Three: Now draw your attention to others. Have it so that behind you are people in general and to your sides are those whom you love and care for. Again, place the women on your left and the men on your right. Think of their pain and confusion. As you breathe in and out, repeat for them what you did for yourself. In your mind's eye, see their negativity come out of their bodies and minds and enter into that place in your heart where such negativity gets dissolved. It can be helpful to visualize this negativity as being like black tar or smoke. As you breathe out, see the radiant clear light spread into their bodies and minds, filling them with clarity, joy, and love.

Step Four: Now think of those you're having particular difficulty with at this time. Imagine that they are sitting directly in front of you. Do the same for them as you did for those in step three.

Take your time building up your strength and resolve to do this practice. Start with yourself. Include others gradually until you can feel comfortable with bringing into your meditation those with whom you have difficulties. Especially with this last step, take whatever time you need in order to develop the equanimity to include someone problematic. Again, as Pema Chödrön teaches, we have to start where we are.

Tong Len can be done on the spot in situations where there is pain or difficulty. Perhaps you're with a friend who is deeply troubled. Or, maybe you're with someone who is feeling hostile toward you. In this person's presence, you can easily breathe in and breathe out in accordance with this practice without his or her even knowing what you are doing. And no doubt, as you hold the intention of wanting to absorb rather than react to the pain, suffering, or bad feelings, this will have an effect on how you relate to the situation. In a hostile situation, it may even quickly dispel the tension or bring it to a resolution more quickly than you had imagined possible.

"DON'T KNOW" MIND—OPENING TO OTHERS

I have had the good fortune of sitting two three-day retreats with the Venerable Seung Sahn, a remarkable teacher of Korean Zen. In his meditation instructions during these retreats, he would encourage students to work with their breathing and pose to themselves the following question: "Who am I?"

As we breathed out, the answer we were to give ourselves was "Don't know."

Much of his teaching through the retreat and in individual interviews was devoted to working with "Don't Know" mind. In effect, the purpose of such instruction was to help us to suspend our opinions about ourselves and who we think we are in the world; thus, we remain natural and open. Knowing ourselves is not about creating and holding on to concepts and constructs, but rather about experiencing and living out of our loving nature without contrivance or expectation.

Since those retreats, I periodically sit and practice in this manner. I find it particularly useful to do this meditation when I'm getting a bit too proud or smug and catch myself feeling aloof, distant, or disconnected from the people I'm with or a situation I'm in—whenever I am having a problem with intimacy. When this happens, I breathe in the question "Who am I?" Breathing out, I say to myself, "Don't know." In this simple practice, it is possible to see cracks in the veneer and begin the process of reaching out in a more authentic way. I come off my high horse and remove my protective veneer so I can walk side by side with my Beloved.

PASSIONATE VISUALIZATION—CHANNELING
PASSION INTO INTIMACY

When we're sitting still, practicing one form or another of meditation or contemplation, we become aware of an entire rainbow of feelings present in our experience. In many instances, these feelings grab our attention and pull us down one road or another. This is especially true for strong feelings, such as anger, jealousy, and, perhaps most of all, passion.

In classic Buddhist literature, there are endless discussions and recommendations on antidotes to dealing with strong emotions, both generally and within the context of meditation. However, I have never seen a text that addresses passion or lust beyond discussing the notion of attachment and—a classic Hinayana approach—suggesting that we create an image of our body or the body of the person we desire in terms of pus and filth in order to move us quickly away from those thoughts.

In the Vajrayana tradition there are meditations that involve seeing ourselves in sexual union with a particular deity, circulating the energy between the visualized form and ourselves in order to bring us to a state of wisdom and bliss. Thus, sexual energy is activated and utilized for a higher spiritual purpose.

Taking this approach as a lead, I offer the following imagery exercise. I did not learn it from any particular teacher, but it is in keeping with Buddhist Tantric practice. It assumes that you're already doing some form of meditation already. Despite the fact that this is not a traditional exercise, I offer it to the reader as a meditative antidote to dealing with strong desire that arises while meditating.

Let's say that I am doing a formal meditation and my mind begins to take a more passionate or lustful direction. I think of my Beloved and I long to be with her. What I have found useful when I am unable to shake my attachment using other traditional meditation antidotes is to imagine the person I long to be with as a female Buddha—which, when properly seen, she actually is. I visualize myself in full sexual embrace with her as is depicted in Tantric iconography and circulate the energy between us. (A full description of this technique can be found in the Tantra section of chapter 8.)

The effect I have observed from doing this practice is twofold. First, as I am not denying or sublimating but rather using these passionate or lustful feelings in a transformative way, I find that I am able to bring myself back into my meditation more wholeheartedly and with more clarity and inspiration than when I began. I feel more balanced and at peace, yet with the added sense of bliss. Second, as I resist any rigid attempt to view my feelings for my Beloved to be a distraction from my spiritual life, my commitment to and appreciation for the richness she brings into my life deepens. I intentionally open up to her more fully.

Such intentions are never wasted.

3

The Power of Anger in Relationships

Knowing that anger makes me ugly,
I smile instead.
I return to myself
and meditate on love.
—THICH NHAT HANH, *PRESENT MOMENT, WONDERFUL*
MOMENT (P. 66)

Negative emotions, such as anger, jealousy, pride, or greed, feel claustrophobic. They seem so solid and intractable. We find ourselves in their midst, gripped. If there is little insight or no practice or discipline that we can engage in to cut through or transform strong negative feelings, we will inevitably react reflexively and, no doubt, sow future seeds for their return. This is the Wheel of Cyclic Existence, *Samsara,* at its most pernicious. If there is a bit more space around such emotions, cultivated by practices we do now or have done in former lifetimes, we may still find ourselves gripped by these emotions, but we maintain some degree of insight that enables us to step back and wonder how we arrived in the mess we are in and, more important, how we can get out.

The insidious nature of these emotions is that they fit within a gestalt—a highly contrived context with certain causes and conditions that foster their development and growth. We are all too often oblivious to the subtle buildup of the situation. Only when we enter the intense feelings we wish we could crawl away from do we finally begin to really pay attention. And by that time, finding our way out in a manner that is not solely determined by habitual response can seem virtually impossible. Caught in our own feelings of being hopelessly ensnared, like a deer in car headlights, we succumb to the self-created chain reaction that follows. In dismay, we try to bandage our feelings of impotency about doing anything different with rationalizations and justifications: "What do you expect?" "I'm only human." "They deserved it." "Wouldn't you have done the same thing?"

Perhaps, if we are at all insightful and honest, and if we can keep remorse from lapsing into guilt and self-denigration, we can at least admit to ourselves that we just couldn't help ourselves—we didn't know how. From the standpoint of current pop and media-driven culture, which makes its money by glorifying drama, confusion, pain, and the endless pursuit to get even, rarely if ever do we see models of people or heroes who are contemplative and sensitive in their approach to working through life's inevitable messes—let alone learn methods we can emulate. And so, why should we expect to know how to help ourselves?

Is there a way out?

Condensed to its most essential purpose, this is exactly what Buddhist practice is about. It reminds us of our loving nature and provides methods to cut through and transform negative emotions and our reactions to the experiences and predicaments they create. Buddhist practice breaks down the seemingly solid walls that reinforce our internal claustrophobia and, in that process, opens us up to working with the energy these emotions inherently possess in a way that is fresh and liberating rather than cyclic and destructive.

Buddhist practice breaks down the seemingly solid walls that reinforce our internal claustrophobia and, in that process, opens us up to working with the energy these emotions inherently possess in a way that is fresh and liberating rather than cyclic and destructive.

Of all the negative emotions, the Buddha taught that anger is the most destructive. It has been said that acting from anger destroys virtue. It certainly destroys good feeling and undermines our connection to our loving nature in the short—and even the long—run. With a single act of anger or rage, the bridges we've created in opening up to and connecting with our Beloved or other loved ones can be damaged irreparably, or it may take a long time to reforge and replace them. If we are at all self-aware, each of us will note that after an angry outburst we feel flat and drained of energy. The stronger the explosion, the longer these feelings persist.

In recent years, modern Western psychotherapy has noted the destructive force anger has when repressed—pushed down deep inside us. The results can be self-destructive attitudes and behaviors that elicit psychosomatic responses, the cause behind any number of chronic and degenerative diseases. Pent-up anger can explode like a volcano. Often, a small irritating incident precipitates an eruption of violence toward others that is disproportionate to the circumstance and may be totally unintended in retrospect—the proverbial straw that broke the camel's back. And so, therapists work on supporting clients to get their anger out in more "appropriate" ways. However, without insight or the awareness that there are potentially liberating qualities behind anger (qualities that we shall discuss shortly) that cannot be accessed through the actual display of anger itself, little is achieved. Some forms of contemporary psychotherapy have mostly succeeded in creating a class of "therapized" people who are relatively intolerant, have "boundary issues," and are fearful of intimacy. Lama Ole Nydahl once commented that if you want to know whether expressing anger is good or not, look at the life of an old psychotherapist and that of an old Buddha.

WRATH VERSUS ANGER

Before going any further on the subject of anger, we need to distinguish here between *anger* and *wrath*. For there is a world of difference.

The Buddha taught that there are four types of compassionate acts: pacifying or peaceful, enriching, magnetizing, and wrathful.

Most of us think of compassion as the state of being peaceful and loving. Indeed, this is the most recognizable form, as when someone approaches us with an unconditional love that settles our mind and allows us to trust our loving nature more. However, we sometimes need to be more empowered. We need someone to enrich us and help us feel our worth, our value, our power. Other times, we may need to be seduced, to be magnetized by someone or something that coaxes us along, giving us a taste of what is possible. And last, though it may seem an unlikely form of compassion, there are times when we need to be confronted or pushed over the edge with a touch of wrath.

Appropriate wrath has a protector function. In the Buddhist pantheon, wrathful deities sometimes confront us, stopping us in our tracks like a mother who slaps the hand of a child who's about to touch the flame on a stove. There are times when the stakes are just too high and the results of a careless act would be more devastating than the intervention. Then there are times when we actually have the capacity for change but remain hesitant, in which case the wrathful deity sneaks up behind us and pushes us off our self-created precipice of safety. In both cases, the wrathful deity is no more than a fierce manifestation of compassion. Mahakala, the squat, dark, bone-crunching, blood-covered, wrathful god is none other than the gentle, compassionate Chenrezig or Avalokiteshvara (Loving Eyes) Thus, wrath, at its root, is love. And what precedes a wrathful act is the experience of love.

This is not the case for anger.

THE MIRROR OF ANGER

Based on who we are and how we've come to see the world through the lens of our own Three Poisons of ignorance, attachment, and aggression, we go through a certain mental process every time something happens to us. In a nutshell, we either like, dislike, or feel neutral about what is happening to us. In turn, whichever of these three reactions we have elicits from us responses to get more of what we like (creating deeper attachment), push away what we don't like (creating stronger aversion or aggression), or just walk right past it as if it didn't exist. When we are unconscious of the habitual cascade of this mental process, we find ourselves haplessly reinforcing our reality without question. We may not even like or want the outcome we're creating, but we feel no ability or power to change what seems to be an unalterable course. The more conscious we become of this process, the greater the likelihood that we will be able to respond—to truly choose a new course—rather than react to the flow.

When we are unconscious of the habitual cascade in our mental process, we find ourselves reinforcing our reality without question. The more conscious we become of this behavior, the more likely we will be able to choose a new course.

Whenever we react to a given situation, we are acting habitually in accordance with our Three Poisons. In choosing new responses, we become the masters rather than the victims of our destiny. As masters of our destiny, we develop an ability to respond based on being in touch with the wisdom inherent in any given situation. There are five types of wisdom, according to Buddhist psychology, that are an expression of our connection to our loving nature, of our living in the experience of our loving nature. These are (1) equalizing wisdom, where we have transmuted the negative emotions of pride and greed, (2) all-accomplishing wisdom, what Robert Thurman also calls "wonder working wisdom,"[1] which is the transmutation of the negative emotional state of envy, (3) individuating or discriminating wisdom, whereby we transmute the negative emotions of lustful passion and conceptualizing everything in our world, (4) all-pervasive or ultimate reality wisdom, which is the transformation of ignorance, and (5) mirror-like wisdom, which is the transmutation of the delusional mind that gives rise to anger.

According to Buddhist tradition, anger is a neurotic manifestation of mirror-like wisdom. When we experience anger in a given situation, what is being mirrored back to us is the claustrophobia inherent in our relationship to that situation. We don't understand the person involved or the situation fully. What we're being confronted with is the unhealthiness of that situation; we're being shown the limitations we've put on our relationship or the narrow boundaries we've enforced and guarded in our undertakings. In other words, our attachments and fixations are being challenged. A larger worldview is beckoning.

When we are angry, we go through stages of fear and anxiety, wishing our conflict would go away without our having to put the effort into making the situation any different—or wishing at least it would comply with whatever borders or boundaries we have previously felt comfortable with. When these wishes aren't granted, we find ourselves not in control. Standing before the mirror a bit more naked and vulnerable than we like, we lash out. We smash the mirror, thinking that if we just destroy the image of our nakedness or vulnerability, we can go back to business as usual, pleasantly dozing in our illusion of safety. What we fail to recognize is that the mirror we have smashed was the source of our clarity and inspiration in the first place. For even in the face of anger, the mirror reflects our vitality. Within our vitality is our power, our creativity, and our possibility. Our vitality is what gives us the spark to embark on new adventures, take risks, leap into the void, lift our sights to new horizons. Whenever we open up to a situation or person in our lives, when we risk beyond our self-imposed limitations, what gets mirrored back to us is the dynamic, playful expression of our loving nature.

> *Whenever we open up to a situation or person in our lives, what gets mirrored back to us is the dynamic, playful expression of our loving nature.*

Realizing the inherent destructiveness in anger, the Buddha was adamant in encouraging people not to lash out with it. Rather than repress these feelings, however, he suggested ways for suppressing them. The difference between repression and suppression is that repression is based in denial, such as when we refuse to honestly acknowledge how we really feel and attempt, instead, to act or behave in a way that we think will be more acceptable to others. When others actually see what is behind the happy face we are putting forward or whatever is lurking beneath the surface, we may get defensive. Over time, if we still continue to live in denial of our true feelings, our original irritation may not only be revealed, it may also now have matured and blossomed into anger—and resentment to boot. With suppression, however, we acknowledge fully what is there and then try to find a means by which we can diminish—rather than bury—the sting. With suppression we utilize the energy of the emotion so that it doesn't get all bottled up. Examples of suppressing emotions include taking time (counting to ten, even if it means ten years) and space (going for a walk or moving out of town). There is no denial of the feelings, but rather an acknowledgment that, in the moment, where we are now, we don't have enough detachment to work with the situation clearly.

Another form of suppression suggested by the Buddha is using the energy of anger to do something that makes us happy or inspired. The Venerable Khenpo Karthar Rinpoche used to say that, in the midst of overpowering anger, meditation can sometimes make matters worse. It is more useful to put flowers on an altar or do something nice for someone else.

MENDING FENCES

Not afraid to be a fool . . .
—THE VENERABLE CHÖGYAM TRUNGPA RINPOCHE

But what of those situations where we just can't help ourselves? Neither suppression nor repression works. The anger just oozes out of us, poisoning our environment and everyone and everything it touches. Maybe we even lash out at the one person we love the most. What then?

Often when we handle a situation badly, we cover up our embarrassment with rationalization and justification, believing that if we make ourselves feel all right with the mess we've made we will also somehow be vindicated in the eyes of others. Recognizing the futility of such endeavors, we need first of all to stay with our embarrassment, our foolishness. We stand in the midst of our foolishness and acknowledge our actions for what they are: uncontrollable, habitual, knee-jerk reactions; nothing more than conditioned responses, like the salivating of Pavlov's dogs.

Second, we need to feel a sense of regret and remorse. We wish we could put the spilled milk back in the bottle. But, spilled milk is spilled

milk. We should not shy away from the sadness that comes with recognizing the pain and suffering we've inflicted upon both others and
ourselves. Staying within the heart of these feelings, we make a commitment to ourselves that, should similar circumstances arise, we will
try to do better. This is a far cry from guilt, in which we take all the
resulting bad feelings from what we have created and flagellate ourselves with them, turning in on ourselves, thus becoming even less
available to connect with others.

Third, and in keeping with our sense of regret and remorse, we
find a means to purify ourselves of the habitual patterns that initiated
our angry outburst in the first place.

For those of you familiar with Tibetan Buddhist tradition, there is
the practice of Diamond Mind (in Sanskrit, *Vajrasattva* and in Tibetan *Dorje Sempa*), a primary method suggested for this purpose.
Dorje Sempa is the bodhisattva who performs the activity of the Buddha Akshobhya, or the Buddha of mirror-like wisdom. The visualizations and mantras associated with Dorje Sempa help to clear our minds
of unhealthy projections so that we can experience our mirror-like
wisdom.

As we meditate on the form of Dorje Sempa and recite Dorje Sempa's
mantra, we imagine that the archetypal sounds of each mantra syllable
stream through our consciousness and body, filling us with a clear nectar that helps to push out disturbing thoughts and feelings; these exit
through the lowest chakra or energy vortex of the body in the form of
smoke, pus, and other unpleasant things. These negativities dissolve
back into the natural elements or are eaten as food by those beings who
would otherwise attack the meditator to feed on the negativities within
him or her. With these negativities eliminated, the body is filled with
pure, clear nectar—the result being a sense of wholesomeness and clarity. This is a Vajrayana meditation. If you are inclined to pursue this
practice and want to receive the full benefit of what it offers, I encourage you to seek out a qualified dharma teacher.

Of course, most cultures and religions have their own styles for
cleansing and purification. Whatever the approach, we must open

ourselves up and become more conscious of our mental and emotional processes by breaking up the solidity of our Three Poisons. With greater space and clarity, we stand a much better chance of catching ourselves before we get too far along the road to turn back.

Last, we make amends if that is possible; we make efforts to rebuild our connection with the one who stood in harm's way. Often we mistakenly try to do this first, apologizing profusely, begging forgiveness, even trying to buy forgiveness. But, without allowing ourselves to experience the sting that has weakened both us and the other, and without transforming our own habitual patterns, more than likely all we create with premature apologies is a sentimental, enmeshed, codependent relationship in which both parties are too numb to examine the cause properly and both try to conjure some other feeling to mask the hurt—at least for the time being. With no real or honest attempt at resolution or deeper insight, we inevitably invite an endless chain of similar situations and responses into our lives. Thus, while we may wish to acknowledge and apologize for what we have done, the sincerity and power behind such words will seem precarious at best until we look more closely at ourselves and begin the essential work to truly eliminate our destructive behaviors. A premature acceptance of apology from the other may encourage us to delay this work.

We must also accept in this matter that sometimes amends are not possible. The relationship we once had may be gone forever. We can decide for ourselves how we are going to be from now on. Our wish to amend what has gone sour is firmly rooted in acceptance, regret, and remorse, and we may be working hard at purifying our minds and emotions of what we have done. We fully and truly are sorry. Nonetheless, we have no control over whether or not the one we have violated with our anger is willing or even able to come to a new understanding of the relationship. Space and time may be what's needed. Maybe the other needs to go away and think matters through. Maybe he or she just wants to go away, and that is that. Space and time will tell.

Although I mentioned earlier that Venerable Khenpo Karthar Rinpoche recommended not using meditation at times when anger is at its most claustrophobic, meditation does nonetheless have a place as an antidote to anger. All of the techniques we mentioned in chapter 2 are indispensable in dealing with anger and all negative emotions we experience. With respect to anger, they help to transform not only the anger itself, but also the dullness it leaves us with. More important, they build up the positive qualities of clarity, openness, and connection with our loving nature, thus making us more immune to succumbing to anger in the first place and falling into the negative vortex created by anger unleashed.

With Calm Abiding, as we feel more at ease with ourselves, we feel more at ease with all our emotions and learn to give them space, whether they are positive or negative. We no longer get seduced or engulfed by them. There is more room to move.

In Tong Len, we become more aware of the sensitivity and pain of others and learn to take back our own projections that limit our appreciation of who they are. We see how unreasonable it is to give them a hard time. In solitary moments during difficult times with our Beloved, friends, and others, we can visualize them sitting beside us, sharing the good feelings of our meditations, and in so doing we transform the energy between us.

Such approaches may seem theoretical or fanciful to those who haven't experienced them. In truth, their transformative power should not be underestimated. To illustrate this point, I would like to share a personal angry moment that happened more than twenty years ago in the early days of my marriage.

When looking back at an angry episode, it is often difficult to detect the subtle crescendo of other feelings that led up to our being in the experience of anger. In this particular incident, I cannot recall what it was that precipitated the cascade of feelings bringing me to anger. However, what made this incident distinct and pivotal in how I would, in the future, handle angry feelings is the space I experienced around the feelings that were building; this space enabled me to know that I was tumbling head-on into becoming angry. I had never known or felt such space around emotions before this time. Then again, I had by then been intensely involved with the practice of Calm Abiding and other Tibetan meditations, and the space I was experiencing felt similar to the space I experienced in my practice. This doesn't mean to say that I maintained a calm or equanimity. What felt absurd to me was that even with this experience of space and the awareness of the subtlety of the buildup of emotion I still did not have enough presence or skill to divert from where I seemed to be heading.

Melanie and I were upstairs in our bedroom. She was on one side of our bed, folding some clothes. I was on the other side. She had her opinion about whatever we were discussing. I had my opinion. Between these two opinions there was a gulf that both of us felt uncomfortable with. And so we baited each other, both unwilling to budge, only willing to win.

As my blood began to rise, I could barely hear what she was even saying. The thought went through my head, "We don't argue upstairs. We argue downstairs in the living room." As ridiculous as this may sound, it was part of the gestalt in which our anger was acted out.

I would like to suggest to the reader that this is how any emotion arises and is supported and sustained. By sheer force of habit, certain feelings arise in certain times and places (or reasonable facsimiles thereof) more frequently than in other times and places. We feel secure and the world seems right and natural when emotions come out in the "right" circumstances. How often do we hear ourselves or others say, "Not here, not now," or "This is not the place," or "This just doesn't feel right here." Sometimes in unfamiliar situations, we may even have feelings we are not able to identify because the time and place do not support their acknowledgment and expression. Later on, back in our lair, we suddenly have insight as to what was going on. And now, in their rightful place, the feelings arise as latent emotional baggage we have carried from one location to another.

As contrived as this thought of place seemed at the time, I was amazed to watch as my wife walked past me, out of the room, and down the stairs to the living room where we normally argued. And, like a good Pavlovian dog, I followed. We baited and taunted each other all the way down the stairs until we arrived at the proper destination for the slugfest to really begin.

When we argued, each of us had our place in the room. Melanie would position herself so she could pace back and forth between the windows and the fireplace. I stood in the doorway to the living room, both guarding her escape and preparing for mine, out the front door just behind me. As she paced to and fro, I would weave back and forth inside the doorway.

Baiting turned to sniping. My wife would mutter something under her breath that I could not exactly make out. I would snap back that I couldn't hear her, at which point she would shout something that was intended to hurt me, but that was obviously shorter than what she'd been muttering. I would try to be cool, rationalizing and neutralizing whatever she said, then countering with something clever and condescending that would make her blood boil even more. This would initiate more muttering, snapping, sniping, and cleverness.

Somehow, I was watching it all as it happened, wondering how the hell we'd gotten to where we were at this moment and feeling totally powerless to say or do anything that was not in compliance with this bizarre habitual script.

Meantime, the lines we recited went faster and our pitch grew more shrill. Her snipes below the belt, a testimonial to all my inadequacies, were now aimed higher—at the jugular. We were locked in deadly combat. We were coming to the moment when, suspending my clever condescension and defensiveness, I would unleash my fury, saying the worst possible thing I could think of at the time. My ploy was to deliver this as I reached back for the inside handle of our front door. I would choose my moment, aim straight, and spew venom. With the final exclamation point flying toward my wife, I would turn, walk through the door that was now partially open, slam it, and go walk around the block. Then I'd come back to the front door where I could hear her crying inside, walk in, and comfort her. We would both feel so wasted by the ordeal that neither of us would really look closely at what had happened. This guaranteed that the pattern would remain intact for future skirmishes and all-out battles.

And there I was, at the front door scene, weapons cocked and ready, watching the fury of her pace wind to a halt as if she was waiting, like a sitting duck, for the final salvo. Then all at once, something changed. I paused, closing the front door as I spun around full circle, looked right at her and said, "Let's go to dinner!"

"What?" she shouted.

"Let's go out to dinner," I said, as the anger began to break up inside me and gave way to exhilaration.

Likewise, Melanie's face and body changed. Startled and joyful, all she could exclaim was, "Great idea!"

A pattern had been broken, one that had often left us devastated for days. I had learned the pattern well from my own parents. They were my feelings, my anger, but each of us learns through conditioning how to play such feelings out. Then we get trapped in the habitual script.

Developing the insight and ability to alter the course of thoughts and emotions from the habits we have built up over years and life-times is no small task. Other than during disasters, which disrupt our lives, rarely do we take the time to question what or how we think. We just want to get on with it—regardless of whether the drama we are in feels good or bad. This is why history, both collective and personal, tends to repeat itself. Knowing this, the Buddha and other teachers and masters since the beginning of time have learned, perfected, then taught methods to break up the cycle of our perpetual confusion before it reaches the disaster level. The wisdom traditions of the world exist for us to be able to intervene in the course of our lives and redirect our efforts toward nobler, more fulfilling ways of being. The Buddha said that to have the opportunity to learn such methods and practice them is as rare as the likelihood of a tortoise swimming up from the bottom of the ocean and managing to stick its head through a floating yoke.

> *The wisdom traditions of the world exist for us to be able to intervene in the course of our lives and redirect our efforts toward nobler, more fulfilling ways of being.*

In this light and with a sense of gratitude, I feel confident that what contributed to disrupting the pattern was the discipline of meditation. I remain committed to these practices because I have found that as we transform and release the burdens we have carried since beginningless time, other negative habitual patterns emerge. Like layers of an onion, the patterns that we become conscious of, see for what they are, and transform will often have other patterns buried beneath them. We may be less conscious of these deeper patterns and may find them even more intractable—as when fear or sadness is found lurking underneath anger; or when our ways of responding to situations seem virtuous or noble but actually disguise and are supported by a sense of pride and competitiveness. The games of ego can be quite subtle. It is interesting to note that in the progression through the stages of practice in Vajrayana Buddhism, visualization meditations start off being focused on peaceful and gentle representations of the Buddha. The further along one gets, the visualizations become more wrathful. Flowers and rainbows give way to daggers and skull cups full of blood. The reason for this is that as we relax and become more comfortable in just being, we grow sensitive to those aspects of our nature that are less savory and less tamed. The meditation practice provides us the opportunity to become proactive in confronting these aspects of ourselves before they loom up in our lives in potentially more forceful and less positive ways.

The truth of this should not be discouraging, especially as it is part and parcel of life as beings in the Realm of Desire—"spiritual beings having a human experience." To manifest our spiritual nature in our human experience, we have no choice but to face such challenges, to overcome complacency and undo habitual patterns. The encouraging news is that if we meet these patterns with openness and such skillful methods as meditation, as more patterns show themselves, we have the ability to clear them. Once we've transformed a single destructive pattern in a relationship, we gain a certainty that we can transform others, along with the energy necessary to do so. We begin to feel that anything that might arise over the natural evolution of a loving, lasting relationship is workable.

That night we went out to an Indian restaurant and had the best meal and the best time we'd had in months. Our one-year-old daughter was with us, and I paid more attention to her and probably had more fun with her that night than I had given myself space for in a very long while.

Over the years, whenever angry feelings have begun to arise, the lessons of this incident have been immensely helpful. For certain, I haven't always had the skill to transform a situation. But knowing the consequences of anger unbridled and having greater resourcefulness to work with such feelings, I've watched such incidents become fewer, blow over more quickly, and often be transformed through seeing the absurdity of the situation and applying the antidote of humor.

Especially in the raising of teenagers, I remained conscious of acting with a greater sense of space and playfulness. I became aware that when I was feeling angry with my children it often meant that I was responding to an internal realization that I was being lied to. Knowing this, I would relax and tell whoever was trying to pull the wool over my eyes that when they were ready to tell me the truth I would be available. I didn't waste my time and energy on lectures and tirades. Not responding with anger to baiting teenagers can have enormous rewards. Indeed, it helped me to be a better listener and friend and more conscious parent. It also allowed them to feel more confident and comfortable in seeking our help and guidance in very trying circumstances.

There are some who believe that one should not display strong negative emotions "in front of the children." I don't agree with this philosophy, although I do agree that to project such feelings and aggression (either mentally or physically) toward a child directly is very damaging. Since life can be ambiguous, confusing, and exasperating, it stands to reason that all of these feelings are components of any committed relationship. If children are privy to watching their parents or others work out conflicts, they get a full energetic display of tension, conflict, and conflict resolution. If we take the tension behind closed doors and then come out smiling as if nothing happened, children miss out on the process. They learn to keep their tensions within and hide; they never learn the resourcefulness needed to take the tensions through whatever stages they need to go through for resolution. When we as parents are not willing to expose our fragile sides to our children—to look vulnerable and even foolish in front of them—they, in turn, cannot come to terms with their own foolishness. Life then becomes heavy-hearted.

> *If children are privy to watching their parents or others work out conflicts, they get a full energetic display of tension, conflict, and conflict resolution.*

Our daughter, who is now in her mid-twenties, has my wife's tongue, my volume, and an intensity we all share. She's still working through the dramas of her life. In the midst of it all, she does not take all that seriously the hell-raising or fury she displays at times. She has stood witness to the truth that all situations and the emotions they evoke can be transformed—even anger.

At the time of this writing, she is considering a career in international conflict resolution. Is it mere coincidence that my wife is English and I am American?

Part Two

Creating the Relationships You Want

Learning to Trust Your Heart

First Thought, Best Thought.
—THE VENERABLE CHÖGYAM TRUNGPA RINPOCHE

Over the course of the following few chapters, I shall present enduring words of advice given by Buddhist teachers both past and present. All of their comments have been extrapolated and interpreted over the years within the context of numerous life situations. Here we focus on these words of wisdom being of practical use for creating passionate and enduring love and relationships.

To start, we look at the words of the great contemporary master Chögyam Trungpa Rinpoche. We shall look at three situations within the context of his above quoted message "First Thought, Best Thought": finding the right partner, love at first sight, and love over time.

FINDING THE RIGHT PARTNER

When we meet someone for the first time, before we can process, analyze, and judge, there is a "first-hit" experience—a "First Thought." Although brief, it is an exhilarating moment of uncertainty that, because it has not been thoroughly screened and processed, reveals to us our enlightened potential referenced against the backdrop of our everyday world. Korean Zen master Seung Sahn speaks of our "checking minds"—the way we examine things—which in fact distances us from our direct, unfiltered experience. With a first-hit experience, we haven't yet had the opportunity to check anything out, to begin our heady analysis. The feeling that we have of the other arises spontaneously; for this reason, it brings the most significant emotional response we could have toward this person. Is it a good, warm, fuzzy feeling, a feeling of indescribable connection? Or, is it a cool, negative, edgy feeling?

What is the source of such feelings? The freshness of the situation that catches us off guard is similar to what Trungpa Rinpoche refers to as "the gap" that occurs when we are fully centered and present in a moment of meditation. Such moments are true meditation. It is what meditators are encouraged to allow to happen, yet not hold on to. For to do so would only create contrivance, grasping, and so on. In one moment, the absolute (Nirvana) and relative (Samsara) are one, the sum total of all previous impressions coming to bear in the here and now. In the context we are speaking of, we are living in the experience of an authentically original and uncontrived moment.

Can the feelings that arise in this First Thought moment be trusted? Is this first thought truly the best thought? Yes and no. Yes, in that your first thought, that first hit prior to all your judgments and rationalizations, is truly where you are in yourself with what you have learned about this aspect of your life to date. It is a very authentic moment. That first impression, that first thought, is your best thought to date. It is trustworthy in that it is honest. No, in that your first thought is really a *relatively* best thought. If it were absolutely your best thought, it would be a thought devoid of bias or presumption. With that totally, fully awakened thought you would be the Buddha fully manifest—at least for that moment. More than likely, this relatively best thought is a bit tainted with some history, fantasy, and hormones thrown into the mix. Still it is far better to rely upon that First Thought response than to try to get around, disregard, or modify it to suit some preconceived concept that pulls you out of your center and back into the graveyard of assumptions—the boneyard for habitual patterns. Let's look at an example.

When you meet someone for the first time, perhaps your first thought is that this person is trouble. That's what comes up when you don't edit your feelings. But your humanistic, psychologically trained, politically correct mind argues a retort: "You shouldn't be so judgmental!" After all, isn't this person trying his or her best? No one should just be written off like that. You think to yourself, we are all basically good. We all possess Buddha potential. We just get sidetracked now and again, now and again, now and again. . . . It takes time, patience, practice, and a lot of acceptance to help us shed that which prevents us from residing wholly and fully in this basic goodness, our loving nature. You remind yourself that everyone has Buddhanature!

> *It takes time, patience, practice, and a lot of acceptance to help us shed that which prevents us from residing wholly and fully in our loving nature.*

So, you override your relative-truth sensibility (trouble) with an absolute truth (another being with Buddhanature). Bad idea.

You decide to go out on a date. Three months later, you come to the conclusion that, as far as you're concerned, yes, this person is trouble. This doesn't mean that this person is trouble in the absolute sense. But in relationship to you and where you are and what you need in a relationship, that's exactly what the person is. You may even have developed a real appreciation of his or her good qualities, but it still doesn't make this person the right partner for you. The truth is that you can deeply and even unconditionally love someone without necessarily being able to live with that person or tolerate what he or she manifests in behavior and action. There is no contradiction in this, and no blame.

> *You can deeply and even unconditionally love someone without necessarily being able to live with that person or tolerate what he or she manifests in behavior and action.*

What should you do? Let go. Move on, and let the other do the same.

This sounds so easy, but you may find you have to repeat this process again and again and again before you find the right partner for you. This may take a relatively short time or it may take years. Neither is better—in the absolute sense, even though from a relative point of view you'd just like to get on and be done with it. When you learn to listen to and trust your first thought, catching yourself sooner each time you begin to preempt your first thought, you will eliminate the people who don't jibe as well with you much faster from your life. As you get better at this, you simultaneously prepare yourself to experience the other end of the spectrum, love at first sight.

LOVE AT FIRST SIGHT

It is my firm belief that this is how it is—that we do experience love at first sight. First Thought in this case can be whistles, buzzers, or wedding bells. You may feel an instantaneous "soul" connection or an ancient and delicious familiarity.

Just as you preempted that thought of "trouble," you can preempt the thought of "Beloved!" You can miss out on the connection you've been longing to make.

Why is that?

With regard to relationships, the impulse that would naturally lead to greater growth, liberation, and the possibility for romance gets preempted by our thoughts and impressions that pull us toward what is familiar, what is known and safe, even if it does not serve us, even if it is detrimental to our well-being—even if it takes us away from our shot at real, enduring love. Because of our inability to trust our loving nature, we compromise, we settle. From this rocky, infertile foundation can only arise unsatisfactory and inevitably destructive relationships. As in our previous case where we talked ourselves into going out with one more piece of trouble, we have been conditioned to look for and, as a result, always encounter trouble. So, if it doesn't look like trouble, we don't even know what we are looking for or looking at. Our habitual patterns blind us or make us mistrust the possible Ms. or Mr. Right who may be on the phone—or standing right in front of us.

How do we get over this? How do we learn to trust ourselves and leap into the space—and the heat—of our first-meeting experience? We must learn to use First Thought, Best Thought.

Catch yourself. We learn to catch ourselves again and again. Every time we see ourselves turning away from warmth, trying to sabotage affection, we must stop. Don't ask yourself why you are holding back. Just drop whatever you're holding on to and open up.

> *Every time we see ourselves trying to sabotage affection, we must stop. Don't ask yourself why you are holding back. Just drop whatever you're holding on to and open up.*

Trungpa Rinpoche, in his meditation program entitled Shambhala Training, wrote new lyrics to several traditional English tunes. In one of these songs he used the words, "not afraid to be a fool," a phrase I cited previously in the discussion of mending fences in relationships. Put into the context we're speaking of here, this means feeling all the wobbly uncertainty and being willing to stick with it; opening up to move forward. In fact, feeling a bit foolish is a guarantee that we are intimately living in the truth of who we are in the moment.

Will we then close up again? No doubt. What to do? We exert ourselves and make an effort to drop whatever fears and obstacles we're holding on to and open up.

This doesn't sound easy. This sounds like work. It doesn't sound natural. Isn't love supposed to be effortless, natural, spontaneous?

Yes, it is. But years of conditioning, years of denying our first thoughts, have made us mistake what is habitual for what is natural, to mistake impulsiveness for spontaneity.

When we are caught in the circular logic of habitual patterns, what should really be natural is no longer effortless. To not respond with what has become familiar and comfortable causes us to feel awkward, embarrassed, confused, and, most of all, threatened. It's simply not what we're used to. It certainly does not feel very spontaneous. And yet, changing our habitually patterned responses is the first step toward spontaneity—into a new way of thinking, being, and acting.

Impulsiveness pales in comparison to spontaneity—even though it can masquerade as one and the same. Impulsiveness is an attempt to break free from the prison of our habits by abdicating responsibility. With impulsiveness, rather than seeing through and letting go of our attachments to our patterns, we try to skirt the issue by succumbing to a whimsical notion that seems far less stultifying than the habitual pattern itself—a "devil may care" type of attitude. What impulsiveness doesn't take into account, however, is that although our habitual patterns are not very liberating, they are part of our world and how we have put things together to make sense of our world to date. In meditation, a person tries to see the nature of these patterns and gently let them go. As this happens, there is more space for action that is clear and precise. In truth, this is what spontaneity is about. It is both sober and alive. Standing in the middle of our own truth, we find the road suddenly much wider than we imagined, and the steps we take arise from an open heart.

Pay attention. Catch yourself.

Gradually, becoming more aware of our habitual patterns, we learn to step back from fourth thought to third thought, from third thought to second thought, until we finally arrive at and wholly trust First Thought. Even as we do this, we need to remind ourselves that First Thought is merely our Best Thought for now. Feeling confident in the relative truth of our First Thought experience, we then need to let go of the burden of perfection—in ourselves and others. Only then will we allow ourselves to be vulnerable and open human beings.

We are so hung up on being perfect. Desire for perfection is probably a common human wish and only gets reinforced by materialistic, goal-driven cultures and the dualistically based religions that benignly, patronizingly proclaim that our failures are the result of our being sinners. Generally speaking, and especially for those who are unable or unwilling to look more deeply into this matter, such cultures and religions perpetuate profound dissatisfaction, which leads to perpetual consumption and more and more twisted, repressive morality. A whole mess results, spiraling out of control.

But anyone with a thinking brain realizes that something is a bit fishy; this model isn't based in truth. The Buddha teaches that we are basically good; what I have been referring to as our loving nature is our inherent goodness. Letting go of perfection not only gives us space to learn and grow, it also creates an opening for others to touch us—for there to be a true meeting, person to person, heart to heart. No longer needing to be perfect, we create the opportunity for a mutual appreciation of our intrinsic loving nature. And the love we've been striving to release becomes more and more evident in our relationships.

Letting go of perfection not only gives us space to learn and grow, it also creates an opening for others to touch us—for there to be a true meeting, person to person, heart to heart.

Can we eventually fall in love with everyone? Actually, and in the most ultimate sense, yes. As in the quote from Gampopa in the Introduction, "It is the sign of a superior man that he treat all with equanimity. . . ." We can ultimately find ourselves loving all with impartiality. Still, in all likelihood, there will be a special someone—a "true love," a "love at first sight."

Some of us may need to go in and out of many relationships to find this special someone. Using First Thought, Best Thought as a rule when meeting others allows us to cycle through these encounters more easily. We learn from each episode and take those lessons into the next. This includes acknowledging those whom we have known as "trouble" in this process. For without their presence in our lives, we would not grow and open to our loving nature. The Tibetans say, "View obstacle as opportunity." Usually what wakes us up most is an obstacle, a detour, someone giving us some trouble. In that light, the Buddha teaches us to always be thankful to whomever we encounter. Trouble, yes. Live with them? Absolutely not! Honor them for the opportunity they have afforded you, but remember to move on.

Whatever our process may be and however long it may take to come closer to and better trust our First Thought, love at first sight is eventually inevitable. Then again, it may have already happened, in which case we can still act on it. Realizing a true bonding relationship from this meeting may or may not be possible, but if it is "meant to be," I don't believe it is ever too late.

In our Western culture, not faced with arranged marriages, we may certainly feel familial and societal expectations, but we are relatively free to make our choice of mate. The field is wide open and we are burdened with options—what I call the tyranny of excessive freedom. In our ever homogenizing melting-pot reality, because there are no specific societal precedents or clear expectations, we have no choice but to trust ourselves, to trust our loving nature. Our First Thought may be our only salvation. I believe that it is.

Will this cause confusion and anguish? Probably. But it's important not to shut down. First Thought, Best Thought is the best antidote to our relationship quandaries as they arise. It is very ecological and efficient. It enables us to make smaller messes and clean them up more effectively. And it will help you recognize that true love at first sight.

LOVE OVER TIME

How does First Thought, Best Thought work in a committed relationship?

Any time we connect with another person, for better or worse, there is an initial spark that draws us together into relationship. From this perspective, "committing" to a relationship involves defining the relationship as the context in which we both do our own work and support the other person in whatever process he or she needs to go through to relate to us.

More often than not, in the ebb and flow of our life's experience, I believe that we do meet the love of our lives, our Beloved. In the initial intensity of this experience—usually triggered by First Thought, Best Thought—most of us choose to initiate a lifelong bond with this person through matrimony or whatever we construe as the best cultural means for demonstrating lifelong commitment.

If this is so, what accounts for the 50 percent divorce rate? What goes wrong?

It is my observation that what pulls us apart are the circumstances we find ourselves in that draw our attention away from that initial experience of love at first sight. Our cultural milieu does not encourage us to learn methods that develop our inner strength and resourcefulness; instead, it supports an outward focus and strings us along in a spiral of perpetual overconsumption. Distraction becomes a way of life.

Commitment stands in opposition to this distraction. Going deep in a monogamous relationship stands in opposition to playing the field and secumbing to the impulse of seduction. It is challenging to feel the freshness and warmth of the initial spark of love in the face of mortgages, child care, work demands, and the long-legged secretary across the hall or that muscular personal trainer at the club, with whom we have none of these worries. Caught in our own habitual patterns and the natural unfolding of life in the relative world, we come to the conclusion that something is wrong with our relationship to our Beloved. We blame each other, beat on each other, walk out on each other, sue and countersue.

What is strange about people I know who have separated or divorced is that often, in moments of crisis later on in life, be they everyday circumstances or existential moments of angst, they reflect on the fact that a deep love remains for their first committed relationship. The spark is still there. This doesn't necessarily mean that the couple should have stayed together and that the divorce was a mistake. Indeed, it may be that they needed to separate in order to go deeper and learn what relationship is truly about. Again, no judgment. But I have seen people who came back together and others who would, if pride and embarrassment didn't get in their way.

In the end, I come to the conclusion that we are not so far out of touch with who we are. First Thought, Best Thought is, in actuality, a force at play in our lives, whether we align ourselves with the truth of that or not. Not recognizing or fully appreciating the gift of our own insight, we fall prey to our own habitual inability to maintain the warmth and freshness of love at first sight.

It is the momentum of the second, third, and fourth thoughts that creates the habitual patterns we need to break away from over time. The clearing of these patterns—the ability to continually reconnect to First Thought, Best Thought—will allow us to live more comfortably and at peace with ourselves and with others. I do not know if this will change the divorce rate or solve the dilemmas so many face in finding satisfaction in intimacy. Perhaps moving through these patterns is just the labyrinth those seeking to know themselves and others through deep, lasting relationships need to go through.

The Buddha had confidence in our loving nature. He taught that, if offered methods for cutting through habit patterns, we will naturally and effortlessly come to our senses. If our very essence truly is our loving nature, then the Buddhist tenet of First Thought, Best Thought must be the everyday shortcut back to connection with that nature. The more consciously we align ourselves with that nature, the greater the likelihood that even our day-to-day circumstances will do nothing to undermine the connection we have with our Beloved—or the opportunity to meet the one who will be our Beloved.

Opening Up to Possibility

*The Great Way is not difficult for those who
    have no preferences.*

*Do not look for the truth. Only cease to
    cherish opinions.*

—Two sayings from Zen patriarch Sengstan

NOTHING TO LOSE

Sengstan is the renowned Third Patriarch of *Ch'an*, the Chinese name for Zen. He is supposed to have lived around the seventh century, but there is only scant information that would support his being anything more than a legend. What is said of him is that he was a worker and a wanderer, an character whose realization and eloquent, pithy writings have inspired many aspirants and seekers throughout the centuries. Yet, like many great individuals of fact and fiction, his legacy is somewhat suspect. It is said that he had to flee from other Buddhist monks who were jealous of him.

The quote "The Great Way is not difficult for those who have no preferences" comes from the "Verses on the Faith Mind," which is a part of his greater work, *Hsin Hsin Ming,* or *The Book of Nothing.*[1] The Great Way that Sengstan refers to in these famous verses is the Great Vehicle, or the Mahayana tradition of Buddhism.

What distinguishes Mahayana Buddhism from the Hinayana or Theravadin tradition is that those who have an affinity with the Mahayana way possess a greater degree of appreciation of Emptiness (or the *Nothing* that Sengstan refers to in the title of his work). What Emptiness is, ironically, is expounded upon in numerous texts and commentaries. As mentioned at the end of chapter 1, and as taught by Lama Ole Nydahl, one of the distinguishing marks of a person who comprehends or has some appreciation of Emptiness is that he or she actually has the capacity to think of the welfare and well-being of others. Understanding the way things are (or dharma)—being less caught up in illusion and our own attachment to and defense of our own position or preferences—we see the world opening up, and through our loving nature we joyfully connect with those around us with little regard for the boundaries between ourselves and others. Opening up fully to who we are, we find that we have nothing to lose. We find ourselves living immersed in an ocean of love with limitless possibilities. This is the ultimate Buddhist view—the view of someone totally identifying with and being part of a very sacred world.

> *Opening up fully to who we are, we find that we have nothing to lose. We find ourselves living immersed in an ocean of love with limitless possibilities.*

On a personal and intimate relationship level, the words "The Great Way is not difficult for those who have no preferences" from Sengstan are useful in several ways.

Each one of us has some notion as to whom we would like to meet, fall in love with, and spend the rest of our days with. These notions are usually a blend of an intuitive understanding of who we are and what we truly need, mixed with karmic patterns and proclivities formed over lifetimes of successful and disastrous relationships—i.e., the impressions and habits we have formed relating to our mothers, fathers, sisters, brothers, and lovers since beginningless time. Because we are conditional creatures, we will inevitably have preferences. We don't want people in our lives who irritate us; we prefer those whose company we enjoy. This is only natural.

But sometimes these preferences can be too strong and particular. The list of conditions—the criteria by which we measure our potentially acceptable suitors—is excessive. We want someone who is tall, dark, and handsome. We want a former cheerleader who is blond and beautiful, with a 34D cup size. We want a passionate lover who is also kind and gentle, or someone who is financially independent, has a strong stock portfolio, and doesn't expect us to cook. We can only be with someone who meditates, likes a particular incense, and has arranged his or her house in perfect Feng Shui balance.

In a relative, ambiguous world, there is no way any one person will meet all of our criteria. Life is definitely untidy in this regard. In fact, we do get what we need in life; but this is absolutely no guarantee that we get what we want. For wants can always be so much larger than needs.

How can you get what you want? Don't make your list of preferences too long. The longer the list, the greater the disappointment. We must be able to prioritize what matters and what is not all that important. Appearances may attract us or put us off. In any case, they inevitably change—regardless of how many procedures involving lasers, liposuction, or implants we decide to endure to freeze-frame a perfect look. Aging affects us all differently; diseases and mishaps along the way may alter our appearance and how we function physically. We may find someone with a compatible lifestyle who seems easy to live with, but the things we do or don't agree upon can change over time with exposure to new and different experiences. Even if we love everything the other person loves, there is no certainty that in five or ten years both of us will still want to sail, golf, and eat Italian food. We may have great intense, passionate sex and think, "Wow! Forty to fifty more years of this!" But then come children, taxes, a swollen prostate, and passion takes a back seat or needs to be approached in a different way. Even at the fundamental level of shared spiritual focus or worldview, we can have huge shifts in perception as life experiences give us new insights. Sometimes these insights bring us closer together; at other times they divide us and we go through periods of feeling isolated and alone—even in the best of company.

The simple truth is that none of these factors ultimately matters when it comes to choosing a partner. Some of our preferences in a partner may be more important to us than others, but in the long run, these preferences are just the context for the relationship, not the relationship's content. If we place too much value on any of these details, then we will end up devaluing what does really matter—the intimate bounding of two souls.

The most successful way to enter a relationship is by letting go and being more relaxed; by developing tolerance, patience, generosity, and above all equanimity. This doesn't mean going along with whoever passes by and expresses an interest, or having babies with anyone we date. Rather, with greater flexibility, we learn to rely on the intuition inherent in our loving nature and not on our conditioning. By fully accessing our loving nature, becoming the warrior the Venerable Chögyam Trungpa Rinpoche spoke of earlier—the one with a strong backbone and a soft, vulnerable front—we can tear up our wish list and open up to possibility.

Thus far, we have looked at the issue of preferences with respect to what we want in another. But what about our preferences with regard to ourselves—what we prefer to do, what we like, how we choose to use our time?

It is one thing to suspend our judgment of another and allow him or her into our life. But what are we willing to give up in order to achieve a greater intimacy? What if there is something we do that keeps the other from being able to relate to us in a positive way?

In the process of opening up to one another, we inevitably find that boundaries become blurred and our definitions of personal space and territory are altered. "My world" becomes "our world." For certain, there are domains within that unified world that more distinctly belong to one or the other, but these remain functional and fun only if both partners view them in the context of the co-created world and both support these areas of individuality. A night with the boys watching Monday night football or a girls' night out can indeed create space and even stimulate a healthier relationship.

But let's say that your boyfriend or soon-to-be husband doesn't mind your girls' night out but has a really hard time when the girls decide to go to a male strip club. Or what if after being married for five years, your wife objects to your friends coming over for Monday night football, because it keeps your kindergartner all revved up and unable to sleep?

Sometimes our personal preferences in these situations become so habitual as to become traditions that seem sacred in their own right. It is important, therefore, to remember they are just habits; they are not cast in stone, nor are they an irreducible aspect of who we really are. If they create disharmony and friction, are they worth holding on to? In giving them up are we compromising or just reestablishing priorities?

When we compromise, we still hold on to our truth—our position and preference as being what's most important—but acquiesce to our partner's demands or position. In some cases, both partners find some relatively acceptable middle ground that doesn't cause either too much discomfort—yet doesn't yield much joy either. Either approach breeds mediocrity at best and resentment at worst. In a dynamic, loving relationship, compromise is not a sustainable solution.

Instead, we need to ask ourselves, "What is my true priority?"

and make choices based on our answers. These may be tough choices to make, but they help us define our values and priorities. Often, when we do this, we will choose to change our own position in a matter based on the realization that what we are co-creating with our partner is more important to us than our position. We allow our priority of relationship to take precedence over other potential choices. In this manner, we essentially release our attachment to a personal position and preference and remain open to the results. By remaining conscious to the fact that we are making a choice, rather than "giving in," we avoid resentment.

I think this strategy is particularly difficult for those who have found themselves single for many years. Being alone, they have grown accustomed to deciding what to do and when to do it. Everything in their life is a well-greased machine based on their own priorities and preferences. Once another person is factored in, they find themselves dealing with uncontrollable mishaps and a world that just doesn't operate according to their expectations.

In the end, we all have to ask ourselves: if intimacy is what I most want, what choices am I willing to make in order to achieve it?

EXPANDING PERSPECTIVES

The quote "Do not look for the truth. Only cease to cherish opinions," also from the work of Zen patriarch Sengstan, serves as another useful tool for living and loving. It means that we need to be willing to give up the primary importance of our own perspective, our cherished opinions, and risk entertaining what possibilities exist in other perspectives.

> *"Do not look for the truth. Only cease to cherish opinions."*
> — ZEN PATRIARCH SENGSTAN

What we think is going on is seldom what is actually going on; it has more to do with how we're thinking about what is going on. In strictly spiritual terms, there are truths that are absolute. But in talking about these truths, we generally find that it's extremely hard to find a way of verbalizing them that would cause us all to nod our heads and say, "Yes, that's exactly how it is." Each of us, as we live our lives exposed to various situations and circumstances, comes to value certain facets of these truths that are relevant to us and our experience. We are like the fabled blind men feeling the elephant.

Everyone comes to a situation from a different angle, a different perspective. Some perspectives, certainly, are better informed than others. The clearest perspectives embrace or at least take into account other perspectives. This is how we teach one another and help one another to broaden our horizons. However, just as we can't make a horse drink when we lead it to water, if a perspective or truth stands too far outside of someone else's experience or reality, we're only wasting our time in trying emphatically to convince him or her that we're right; at worst, this can become a form of abuse, a denigration of the other person's experience. Here we must be willing to give up the primacy of our own perspective and to stretch ourselves, possibly beyond our own comfort zone. We need to remind ourselves that everyone is doing the best he or she knows how, based on a particular set of life experiences. As everyone possesses a loving nature, there is always something to learn from how anyone has come to see things.

In this way a greater sense of the truth of any situation arises in a very organic way. Instead of ramming our truth down other people's throats, we create an openness, an atmosphere of mutuality, in which it becomes possible for us to value other perspectives and for others to entertain our perspectives as well. The larger truth emerges as a shared experience. The Great Way becomes possible as a living reality—and everyone benefits.

In communication, accuracy does not ensure intimacy. Holding to our opinions as the only truth can only serve to divide and isolate. Sure, we may be committed to certain principles from which we do not wish to stray. However, if we're to include another person in our life, these principles need to be flexible enough to embrace the reality of that other person. Sometimes, of course, we find ourselves trying to combine chalk and cheese. Some things cannot be reconciled from where each person stands. Does such a deadlock mean that the relationship is doomed to failure?

Maybe. Maybe not. A lot depends on the relative value of what cannot be reconciled. But even something important can be set aside or laid to rest for the time being. It is not a cop-out to come to an agreement not to deal with something. For some things will just resolve themselves over the course of life as our perspectives change and our insights deepen. Whatever hasn't resolved itself will assuredly come around again. And it might be that, when it does, both parties have more personal resourcefulness to come to a better understanding, a greater shared truth. This is the gift of long-term relationship—which is even more poignant in an era when instant solutions and quick fixes are the acceptable norm and expectation.

The truths worth embracing that are of any value to us as human beings serve only to bring us together. But this coming together—seemingly so simple in theory—requires each of us to dismantle the Three Poisons of ignorance, attachment, and aggression that create the illusion of our separation from one another. The truth can indeed set us free. But to be free and know how to work with and in the light of truth requires commitment. The weight of this work lightens when we find someone whose commitment to the value of intimacy, as a joyful expression of our enlightenment potential, is equal to our own. In short, this work is manageable with our true love.

A passage by Rainer Maria Rilke that I have recited at weddings for friends most aptly expounds such true love and the higher purpose of relationship. Although he was not a Buddhist himself, much of Rilke's work expresses truths that both Buddhists and people of other spiritual traditions can agree upon wholeheartedly. This is a demonstration of the truth that dharma, the way things are, is non-sectarian or presectarian to those willing to look deeply and love. Here, Rilke manages to demonstrate both our aloneness and how that aloneness is supported and honored in intimacy. From a strictly Buddhist point of view, he conveys the deeper significance and value of what in Buddhism is called *sangha,* or the community upon which a person following the dharma can rely.

> I hold this to be the highest task of a bond between two people: that each should stand guard over the solitude of the other. . . . And only those are the true sharings which rhythmically interrupt periods of deep isolation. . . .
>
> But, once the realization is accepted that even between the *closest* human beings infinite distances continue to exist, a wonderful living side by side can grow up, if they succeed in loving the distance between them which makes it possible for each to see the other whole and against a wide sky![2]

Rilke reminds us of the truth of our existential aloneness juxtaposed with the truth that love is our salvation from succumbing to feelings of loneliness. Our path to the experience and realization of the intimate at-oneness of enlightenment* is our own, and only we can tread that path. However, when we allow friends, and especially our Beloved, to stand beside and inspire us with fresh perspectives and possibilities, the process leading to the full realization of our true potential becomes that much richer.

FOLLOWING THE PATH OF YOUR LOVING NATURE

Sometimes the truths and priorities we are asked to examine when in a relationship strike right to the core of our being as individuals. Each

---

*This concept is explained by Robert Thurman in *The Tibetan Book of the Dead* and is discussed in this book in chapter 1 (page 14).

of us has dreams and aspirations, be they mundane or noble. Based on where we are within ourselves and how we see the world, we know in varying degrees what is possible and what resources we need to achieve these longings. According to Buddhist thought, even dreams and aspirations are an integral part of our karma—which amounts to all the causes and conditions that come together over lifetimes to create the situation of our birth and to precipitate the events and circumstances that unfold over the course of our current life. (See chapter 6 for a more detailed description and discussion of karma.) Our reactions to the events and circumstances we face are also determined by inclinations we have acted upon lifetime after lifetime—what we've already discussed as our habitual patterns.

Buddhist thought teaches that in disrupting our habitual patterns we can develop a detachment that gives us the ability not only to take responsibility for whatever predicament we find ourselves in, but also to have the clarity and openness to choose another course. The purpose of meditation is, in fact, to create the space, what Trungpa Rinpoche calls "the gap," that allows us to awaken to our loving nature and use it more intelligently and with greater precision. We become authentic free agents.

Relationships provide an important key to karmic liberation. When we meet someone and develop a long-term intimate relationship, some of our individual dreams and aspirations lose their relevance. New goals arise for the couple through the energy the couple creates together. But some of the old dreams and aspirations become even stronger because we see that with our mate's support, we stand a greater chance of reaching them, or perhaps through the process of paring down what is most important to us, we have discovered our most pressing priorities. In this way, our relationship focuses the power of each partner, while simultaneously creating a power that is the result of the union. One plus one in this situation equals far more than two. The power of this union becomes the force through which our individual and collective karmas accelerate and more effortlessly resolve.

What happens, though, if your dreams point in different directions? Let's say one of you gets a fantastic job with lots of benefits—the job you always wanted. But the other has always dreamed of studying art and has just received a scholarship to a college in a different town. You've been together as a couple for a long time (however you want to define that) and you hate the prospect of having a long-distance relationship. What do you do?

The Venerable Khenpo Karthar Rinpoche, a contemporary Tibetan Buddhist master living in the United States, once gave me this piece of advice: "Go where the karma is strongest." Over the years, these words have been invaluable for me and have cut through the usual linear rational banter that sometimes gets in the way of acting decisively in an ever more ambiguous world.

> *"Go where the karma is strongest."*
>
> —THE VENERABLE KHENPO KARTHAR RINPOCHE

Khenpo Karthar Rinpoche is not suggesting leaving the relationship. For in the end, after success has come and gone, we are left with each other. And it is the love we have extended each other over the years that will be remembered. Defending the union at all costs is very powerful. Making the relationship the foundation upon which all of life's events and circumstances arise—including our highest dreams and aspirations—honors the relationship as the *axis mundi,* the central nonnegotiable reality of our lives. A union forged with such a view will certainly be dynamic and resplendent with opportunities for development and growth.

So what does it mean, then, to "go where the karma is strongest"? In martial arts, one of the first rules taught is never to meet a larger force head-on. Step aside and the momentum of that force will pass by and take care of itself. Similarly, by stepping aside for our partner's karmic train and allowing it to run its course without resistance, we enable that particular impulse to be honored. The energy of that dream is allowed to come to fruition. The karma is completed. Now our Beloved can move on, and likewise, so can we.

The gift we give our partners in stepping aside, in "going where the karma is strongest," is not just the opportunity to allow them to pursue their dream. It is also the opportunity for them to become more of who they are and who they want to be without all the buildup of shoulds and what-ifs, and the resulting resentments. As in Rilke's words on intimacy and what is truly shared in a loving relationship, we stand witness to and support the unfoldment and development of our Beloved's loving nature. The relationship is strengthened and honored by acting as an accelerating force rather than creating clogged energy that breeds frustration, anxiety, and depression.

Accepting the risks involved in yielding to the greater karmic force in the relationship seems far preferable to remaining entrenched in our own position and preferences. What fuels the relationship in that case is a lack of understanding of its potential power. Then the shoulds, what-ifs, and resentments painfully and gradually or even suddenly destroy intimacy, the individuals, and, in the end, the relationship itself.

When we choose to honor our partner's karmic path with a sense of joy, we have truly learned how to act for the benefit of another. If we feel that we're acquiescing and stand by with smug detachment or indifference, we merely display our attachment to our own preferences. Creating a positive open space for our Beloved's dream to manifest ensures the greatest possible outcome—both for that person's individual growth as well as the growth of the relationship.

If we are committed to developing a lasting, deep, and intimate relationship and approach our dreams and aspirations in the spirit of

Zen patriarch Sengstan's verses and Khenpo Karthar Rinpoche's pragmatic advice for building a closer and deeper relationship, we open ourselves up wholly, unabashedly, trusting that our loving nature gives us the capacity to surrender everything to our Beloved. When we act in this way, not only do we not lose anything, but the benefit the other derives from our giving will inevitably come back around to us. If there is a dream, an aspiration that really matters to you, in the spirit of love and openness that the two of you have created, no doubt your time will come.

Karma: Feedback as Payback

What you are is what you have been, what you will be is what you do now.
—The Buddha (cited in *The Tibetan Book of Living and Dying*, by Sogyal Rinpoche, p. 93)

Karma means *action; an activity, a happening.* When someone does something, there are intended and unintended effects. We do something to get something done and other things happen just because of the fact that we've taken some action. Newton formulated this as "For every action, there is an opposite and equal reaction." We may not see all of what is caused by what we do, as we focus on what we want to get from what we've done. But, over time, we'll get the full effect. The outcome of our actions will return to us in hearts or spades.

Karma is composed of two interdependent aspects: habitual patterns and what Bönpo master Tenzin Wangyal Rinpoche calls "karmic traces," which trigger certain knee-jerk responses. As Tenzin Wangyal Rinpoche states, "Every action—physical, verbal, or mental—undertaken by an individual, if performed with intention and even the slightest aversion or desire, leaves a trace in the mindstream of that individual. The accumulation of these karmic traces serves to condition every moment of experience of that individual, positively and negatively."[1] Owing to circumstances we have found ourselves in since beginningless time, we have developed habitual (knee-jerk) responses to those circumstances that either reinforce or somehow alter—for better or worse—what karmic traces will be set in motion and come to fruition as future circumstances in our lives. As stated earlier, *beginningless time* is a Buddhist concept that implies the cyclic nature of this phenomenon and the fact that there is no beginning point that does not have its own karmic traces as the cause. This cycle of habitual patterns creating karmic traces breeding the karma that triggers habitual responses, and so on in endless succession, is represented in Tibetan Buddhist iconography as The Wheel of Life; this is the cycle of cause and effect, the realm of Samsara.

> *"Every action—physical,*
> *verbal, or mental—*
> *undertaken by an individual*
> *leaves a trace in the mindstream*
> *of that individual."*
> —TENZIN WANGYAL RINPOCHE

In the predicament of life, we cannot change what we are facing once we're in the midst of facing it (no genies allowed!), but we can change how we approach what we are facing. We can make choices that lessen the grip of habitual patterns. This, in turn, sends out different karmic traces, and they, in turn, change what we will face in the future. This is all well and good for the future, but we need to remind ourselves that this does not absolve us in any way from experiencing what we have already set in motion from our previous actions. If you jump off a cliff and have an epiphany that it was the wrong thing to have done and wholeheartedly commit yourself to never making the same mistake again, gravity will still have its way with you.

> *If you jump off a cliff and have an epiphany that it was the wrong thing to have done and wholeheartedly commit yourself to never making the same mistake again, gravity will still have its way with you.*

Karma is not just an Eastern idea. It exists as a religious or philosophical truth in cultures throughout the world. Our Western biblical saying "As you sow, so shall you reap" is about karma. But for some reason, whereas we tend to ignore this as some kind of gratuitous truism or cliché, Eastern traditions place great emphasis on the concept of karma. Perhaps as we have removed the notion of reincarnation from our religious traditions, we have gutted the notion of karma to boot.

> *"With the heavenly eye, purified and beyond the range of human vision, I saw how beings vanish and come to be again. I saw high and low, brilliant and insignificant, and how each obtained according to his karma a favorable or painful rebirth."*
>
> —The Buddha[2]

In the East they look at what people experience now, good or bad, fortunate or unfortunate, as a direct result of what they have done in the past, whether the immediate past in their current life or a past from lifetimes beyond conscious recollection. It's a fact that many life circumstances and events don't necessarily make sense just within the context of what we've done and where we've been in this current life. Without an appreciation of past lives, as we strive to make all of reality fit with the data we gather from this life, we are left to ponder why bad things happen to good people and good things to bad. In the East, there is no mystery here at all. For karma exhibits a mathematical precision that informs how we cycle in and out of existence. Buddhist texts teach that karma is infallible. We never really experience or "get" what we don't deserve in some way.

Sometimes we can see the reasons for what we get in life. Every one of us periodically receives the benefit of "instant karma," an obvious repercussion from something we've just done. Often, however, we seem to get a "bolt out of the blue," so that we may even ask ourselves, "Where did that come from?" This can apply to both the bad and the good, including the fateful meeting with our Beloved.

It's important to understand that in the laws of karma the relationship that seems "meant to be" was literally meant to be. Our soul mate, our Beloved, comes to us through the causes and conditions that ripen at a certain point in time, bringing us together with a knowing that shows the unbroken linkage from one life to the next. However, any such seemingly charmed event in our lives—whether we take credit for it or chalk it up to luck or fate—is ephemeral, a wave in the ocean of life. Sitting back like a fat cat with a bowl of cream can create its own karmic kickback later on. This doesn't mean that we shouldn't enjoy the good that comes to us. What it does mean is that it is always prudent to mix joy with humility and a desire to share the good feelings.

Our Beloved comes to us through the causes and conditions that ripen at a certain point in time, bringing us together with a knowing that shows the unbroken linkage from one life to the next.

But what about those of us who find few cherries in the pits? Try as we might, life's seeming rewards (money, success, relationship) seem to elude us. Seeing karma as always infallible may be a bitter pill to swallow.

With respect to other people, we must recognize that there are neutral or unpleasant relationships that were also meant to be. Being from the Realm of Desire, we feel the heat and joy of the relationships we cherish and respond with a tightening and aversion to those that are doomed to disaster. Without the practice of equanimity and a profound appreciation of karma, we will always be blaming other people or external circumstances; we will never fully grab our individual power and take responsibility for making changes now or in the future.

But nothing is carved in stone. The sands of time can reduce even granite to dust. Unless we embrace the fact that we are able to affect our life's course, the negativity we perpetuate in how we dwell on and react to unpleasant people and circumstances will more than likely be the cause for future disappointment. For karma is not the same as fate or predestination, as many Westerners have tended to view it. Rather, if we have repeated something over and over again, adding layer upon layer of reactions, the thickness or density of this habitual pattern will be the cause for us to repeat the same actions. Karma may explain how we got from where we were to where we are, but it doesn't necessarily have anything to do with where we are going—unless of course we continue to perpetuate that which we're experiencing now by engaging in the same reactions born of habitual patterns. This is in keeping with one of my favorite colloquial sayings: "If you always do what you've always done, then you'll always get what you've always gotten."

> *If you always do what you've always done, then you'll always get what you've always gotten.*

Deep down, we all know this, and in every moment we are conscious to some degree of what we are doing as right or wrong, beneficial or harmful. We know when we're coming from a space of freedom and openness or of stiffness and constraint. When we act in accordance with our loving nature, our body expands and feels lighter. Our mind feels inspired and positive emotions arise naturally; we feel effortless joy, excitement, happiness, love. Conversely, when we do something that runs counter to our loving nature because of the Three Poisons, we contract. We cannot look others in the eye, we feel a constriction in our throat, we become overly emphatic or vague; in short, we experience a growing distance between ourselves and others.

These things are self-evident. Our body, mind, and spirit are wonderful, reliable instruments. Ultimately, they cannot deceive us. We never get away with anything. And the truth is, on an energetic level, we can never really hide anything from anyone else. When we lash out, others feel our fear. When we fake loving words or displays of affection, they feel our deception—even if they can't acknowledge or act on this in the present.

> *"We can never really hide anything from anyone else. We just agree not to blow each other's cover."*
> —KARMA SONAM WANGCHUK

The distance we create with deceitful words or actions will inevitably be a determining factor in how others choose to interact with us in the future. All that happens in the moment is that we tacitly agree not to blow each other's cover. And the degree to which we cover up for each other's insincerities—be they intentional or not—is the degree to which the moment is inauthentic and perpetuates disconnection rather than connection.

That said, we must remember not to be too heavy-handed with ourselves. Changing habitual patterns, loosening the grip of the Wheel of Life, is the primary goal of the meditation methods taught by the Buddha and shared in the chapter on meditation. It is no small task.

For sure, there are some patterns that are easy to change, and when we engage in a process that helps us become more self-aware, they dissolve as if by magic. But there are other patterns that have been practiced for a very long time, and the resulting karma is a thick forest with large, grotesque tree trunks—as when we find ourselves attracting the same types of difficult people into our lives even after years of meditation, therapy, self-assertion groups, and so on.

Such karma and the patterns that are its cause can seem intractable. In truth, though, they are not. Our process of self-discovery is undoubtedly making a difference, though it may feel like various and barely discernible gradations of black. Patience, kindness toward ourselves, persistence, and humor are invaluable prescriptions.

THE WHEEL OF SHARP WEAPONS

Buddhist tradition teaches that with clear, unbiased perception, we would be able to see and understand how our karma has unfolded up to the present moment. However, more often than not we deliberately mystify ourselves with self-deception, hoping that what we create will somehow turn into what we want. Or we get so caught up in the Three Poisons that we literally cannot see the repercussions of our actions—let alone how actions in our previous lives have created the karmic traces determining what we experience now.

Within the Buddhist tradition, there is a powerful and poignant text that clearly elucidates for us why others respond to us the way they do. This text, *The Wheel of Sharp Weapons*, was written by the great Indian yogi Dharmarakshita. In many respects, it serves as a complement to Shantideva's text on the conduct befitting the ideal Mahayana practitioner, the *Bodhisattvacharyavatara*. *The Wheel of Sharp Weapons* was brought into Tibet by the renowned master Atisha, a student of Dharmarakshita's, and by Upasaka Bromtonpa, Atisha's main disciple during the eleventh century. Atisha was especially interested in mind training and the value of developing our loving nature in the course of everyday activity and interaction. In keeping with this emphasis in his teaching, *The Wheel of Sharp Weapons* addresses what happens when we don't act in accordance with Mahayana ideals, what comes back to us as a result, and how we can remedy the situation. Atisha's studies and work, later compiled by Chekawa Yeshe Dorje in *The Seven Points of Mind Training*, provide meditative methods and an elaboration of Dharmarakshita's *Wheel*.

My purpose in sharing excerpts from this text is not to generate guilt. Essentially, Dharmarakshita wanted to wake us up. He wanted us to pay attention to our experience and become more responsible; to commit ourselves to overcoming the Three Poisons of ignorance, attachment, and aggression in order to live consciously and create the karma we want. But this is not achieved through self-flagellation. Accepting where we are and how we got there is the first step in making a commitment to change our course. There are 119 verses and an epilogue included in *The Wheel of Sharp Weapons*. I have elected to present those that represent some of the more common difficulties we may have in our everyday interactions.

> *When all who are close turn against us as enemies,*
> *This is the wheel of sharp weapons returning*
> *Full circle upon us from wrongs we have done.*
> *Till now we have had grudges inside us with anger*
> *With thoughts of sly methods to cause others pain;*
> *Hereafter let's try to have less affection,*
> *Nor pretend to be kind while we harbour aims.*[3]

> *When others find fault with whatever we are doing*
> *And people seem eager to blame only us,*
> *This is the wheel of sharp weapons returning*
> *Full circle upon us from wrongs we have done.*
> *Till now we have been shameless, not caring about others,*
> *We have thought that our deeds did not matter at all,*
> *Hereafter let's stop our offensive behaviour.*[4]

> *When we are born in oppressive and wretched conditions,*
> *This is the wheel of sharp weapons returning*
> *Full circle upon us from wrongs we have done.*
> *Till now we have always had a negative outlook—*
> *We have criticized others, seeing only their flaws.*
> *Hereafter let's cultivate positive feelings*
> *And view our surroundings as stainless and pure.*[5]

> *When our minds are disturbed and feel great frustration*
> *That things never happen the way we wish,*
> *This is the wheel of sharp weapons returning*
> *Full circle upon us from wrongs we have done.*
> *Till now we have caused interfering disturbances*
> *When others have focused on virtuous acts;*
> *Hereafter let's stop causing such interruption.*[6]

When unjustly we are blamed for the misdeed of others,
And are falsely accused of flaws that we lack,
And are always the object of verbal abuse,
This is the wheel of sharp weapons returning
Full circle upon us from wrongs we have done.
Till now we have despised and belittled our Gurus;*
Hereafter let's never accuse others falsely,
But give them full credit for virtues they have.[7]

Dharmarakshita's words are sober and direct. Experiencing harsh conditions, being the victim of verbal abuse, feeling betrayed or frustrated, all are rooted in our previous actions—the yield of what we have sown, whether we're aware of it or not. Further, he calls us to positive action. For neither denial nor retaliation will remedy negative circumstances for us. Trusting and living out of our loving nature in our dealings with ourselves and others is the only solution. This is especially true with regard to those we love and are closest to.

> *Neither denial nor retaliation will remedy negative circumstances for us. Trusting and living out of our loving nature in our dealings with ourselves and others is the only solution.*

JUDGMENT, INTERFERENCE, AND ABUSE

Although *The Wheel of Sharp Weapons* is a wonderful reminder from the heart of the Buddha's teaching, the simple fact is that unless we have transformed the Three Poisons entirely and live and act as a

---

*The word *Gurus* here refers to enlightened teachers and, in varying degrees, to our elders, virtuous people, or kindhearted friends.

Buddha incarnate, it lies beyond our present awareness and comprehension to know fully what our actions or those of others yield karmically. Sometimes actions done with the best intentions create what look like disastrous results, while acts that appear to be totally inappropriate, even downright evil, create seemingly more good than bad. Consequently, judging, especially when it comes to the actions of others, is generally somewhat suspect.

What can be said, however, is that in the moment, based on what we have learned about the world and who we are in it, in seeking what we define as happiness and what will lead to happiness, we are all doing the best we know how.

This doesn't mean we need to like or approve of everything others do. We may feel compelled to challenge or confront them, even stop them in their tracks. What we need to remember is that any judgment we make and the actions we choose in response are, as all else, based on habitual patterns and karmic tendencies. To declare that so and so "deserves" to be treated a certain way is to make a judgment that most of us are unqualified to make.

Great teachers, we should note, are highly skilled in shocking our sensibilities as to what we do or do not deserve. I have seen highly evolved and respected Buddhist masters treat kindly those whom others scorn and treat with indifference those who view themselves (or are viewed by others) as important, wonderfully benevolent people. People who feel miserable about themselves might expect chastisement when face-to-face with such teachers, but instead receive only kindness. Others get shocked back to their senses in the face of a teacher's penetrating wrath—one that bears surgical accuracy. Although there are cases of teachers who abuse their authority, I have for the most part experienced, witnessed, and heard of people who, in the presence of great teachers, receive invaluable lessons about karma. In not acting in an expected or seemingly predictable manner, these teachers help students to become aware of their habitual patterns by not letting events flow on uninterrupted. They get to look directly at who they are and at what they are doing.

While there are moments when we unwittingly or by some moment of spontaneous clarity are able do this for each other, for the most part, such lessons are not for the rest of us to teach. We don't know what others really deserve. Instead, we must hold the awareness that each of us has as our core a loving nature; thus, our judgments of others (and ourselves) are tempered. When we assume responsibility for the actions of others and intercede as a divine arbiter, we are only insulting their loving nature.

A good starting point in our response to another is to find out what his or her intention was. Until we are fully enlightened, it will always be that our actions in the relative everyday world will create unintended and sometimes undesired effects. Given this fact, and given that we're all doing the best we can, intention is the only true marker we can go by in responding to the actions of others. For it is in their intention that we see how closely they are attempting to align their actions to their loving nature. Acknowledging this point first and attempting in our response to be as true to our own loving nature as well—whether we respond with gentleness or wrath—we will act in a way that inspires rather than stifles growth, ours as well as theirs.

"Don't transfer the ox's load to the cow." This is a teaching of Atisha's passed on in *The Seven Points of Mind Training*. Its main point, according to the commentary by the great Jamgon Kongtrul Rinpoche in *The Great Path of Awakening* is that we must take responsibility for our actions and for what we are called to do in our lives.[8] Especially when it comes to difficult decisions, it is unethical and karmically unsound to dump what is ours into the laps of others. When we displace a problem onto another, it obviously creates an unnecessary burden for that person. But for us it also usually means that whatever was trying to get our attention in the first place will have to get larger so that we're forced to take notice and deal with it.

> *Don't transfer the ox's load to the cow. We must take responsibility for our actions and for what we are called to do in our lives.*

From another vantage point, however, this saying is also quite useful when our judgments lead to interference in the path or karma of our Beloved. Whenever we are intimately involved with another, there is a tendency for us to assume we know who that person is, what our Beloved's words and actions mean, and even what he or she needs. These assumptions may or may not be well founded. However, because they are based on historical data—what we have known of the person to date—they will inevitably lead to our limiting our partner's possibilities. Thus, we deny our Beloved the opportunity to step out of his or her paradigm or worldview.

Whenever we step in in some heavy-handed way, we prevent our loved one from trying something new, taking risks, even feeling hesitancy or frustration. We rob him or her of an opportunity for growth. What we achieve, in fact, is the antithesis of what Rilke refers to as seeing our Beloved "whole and against a wide sky." Such codependency may come from the best of intentions—out of kindness and concern— since codependency is nothing more than a neurotic manifestation of our altruistic heart. But what we demonstrate with our interference is a lack of trust; we show that we don't believe our loved one capable of working things out for him- or herself. At the same time, we take over the power in the relationship. Mutuality is lost and, with it, degrees of intimacy.

What happens when our judgments and interference lead to forms of abuse? From our earlier excerpts from *The Wheel of Sharp Weapons*, the repercussions that the perpetrators might experience as a result seem a given, even if we don't know exactly in what shape or form the karmic payback will arrive. However, let us look more closely at this matter from the standpoint of the one receiving the abuse.

When we experience the anger of others, it may well be that, according to our karma, that is what we deserve. However, sometimes the learning curve is too great and what we get from a tongue lashing, a physical threat, or any kind of painful interaction is not a jolt that brings us to our senses or to a new level of awareness. In the face of harshness, we may recoil, shut ourselves down, and withdraw. We may even find ourselves building up thoughts of resentment, retaliation, or even varying degrees of self-denigration. If this is where the situation has taken us within ourselves, it may be prudent and necessary to do whatever it takes to step out and get away from the perpetrators concerned—not only for ourselves, but also for their benefit as well.

Let's say you are a woman living with domestic violence. Your spouse or partner beats you. He says it's because you are a tease and a flirt and that you flaunt yourself at others. Perhaps this is true, perhaps not. Perhaps you know you have the tendency; maybe in a past life you were unfaithful and remorseless. (The Wheel of Sharp Weapons returning?) But now, rather than getting the space from yourself and your partner to let go of this tendency, you develop a sense of self-loathing and buy into his beating you all the time. When he's with you in public, you act timid and awkward—which riles him even more. Maybe you're hiding something.

In the long run, the abuse you are experiencing will never solve this matter nor serve as absolution. It will certainly never bring you and your spouse closer together. The old saying is that "violence begets violence." At the very least, the violence will make you feel worse about yourself and about him. According to the Buddha's teachings, self-denigration is the most insidious and destructive force against our loving nature. Furthermore, your partner is not helping his own karmic predicament either. It's a lose-lose proposition. In allowing or not stepping out of the way of his violence, not only do you weaken your own being, destroying your alignment to your own loving nature, but you are also acting uncaringly toward him.

Well, you say, what about the sweetness of revenge? Shouldn't he get what he deserves?

There is an elegant old Welsh saying that goes "When planning revenge, always dig two graves." It's just a little reminder that we really don't know what others deserve for what they do to us. However, we can know with certainty that what we're getting out of the situation is only bringing out the worst in us. That's when, for everyone's sake, we get the hell out of there!

The point in looking at judgments, interference, and abuse is for us to recognize that in order to develop a positive relationship to ourselves and others, we must first and foremost remember to align our intentions with our loving nature. As we do so, we forge more bridges and create fewer chasms between ourselves and our Beloved.

It's evident that most of us are—to varying degrees—clouded in our abilities to identify with and act from our loving nature; hence, we act selfishly or inappropriately, from emotions such as anger, jealousy, and indifference. This is all testimony to the folly of the Three Poisons, which we as humans experience lifetime after lifetime.

Our words and actions usually fall within a range of being in touch with our loving nature and being caught up in the Three Poisons of ignorance, attachment, and aggression and the delusionary vision they create. The more deluded our perception, the more the Three Poisons will be the source for our behavior. Conversely, the more centered and open we are, and the more in touch with our loving nature, then the more our actions arise spontaneously, effortlessly, as in Trungpa Rinpoche's First Thought, Best Thought.

In this context, even acts that interfere with or seemingly cause a degree of pain to another can come from a relatively more enlightened or unenlightened perspective. What determines whether they create negative or beneficial results is whether they're performed with ego-based deliberateness and willfulness or with altruistic intention.

When we act with altruistic intention, we approach what we do with a particular focus and aim in mind to consciously create a certain beneficial outcome. Such mindfulness implies a flexibility in working with the situation and acts as its own protection, as we become keenly aware when things are going awry. But when we're being willful and deliberate, focusing on meeting our own specific needs, we compound our intention with force or manipulation. Come hell or high water, we want things to turn out the way we want them to turn out. Ego-based willful and deliberate actions disregard mutuality and definitely constitute negative intrusion and interference in the course and karmic flow of the lives of others.

There are times, of course, when force is necessary—usually for some noble reason that benefits others, perhaps teaches a lesson. But, for the most part, even when the best intentions are carried out with force, the karmic fallout is heavy. Though we may achieve what we set out to achieve, our force will create consequences that we cannot ignore. In this case, it is best for our intentions to be pristine.

It may be that Atisha was thinking upon such things when he gave the following advice: "Don't wait in ambush" and "Don't act with a twist."

> *In relationships, don't wait in ambush and don't act with a twist toward your partner.*

In a relationship, waiting in ambush can take several forms. It might occur when we want something from our partners, when we have a point to make, or even when we deliver a judgment about them. We try to catch them when they're least likely to resist: when they're depressed, unsuspecting, or distracted by something else, as when walking out the door or in the middle of making love. Sometimes this is a skillful and necessary tactic. More often, there's an element of cowardice on our side. In any case, such an act is always manipulative.

Acting with a twist is when we have already made a point, but then twist the knife, causing a deeper level of damage. This is willfulness gone berserk and usually has more to do with power than anything else. After we act in such a manner, how should our Beloved respond? And how long does it take before mutuality and trust are reestablished in the aftermath? More than likely, longer than we would have imagined; in some cases, it never happens.

THE BIGGER PICTURE: COLLECTIVE KARMA

Thus far in our discussion, the emphasis has been on individual karma and what we experience as a direct result of what we put in motion. Our individual karma determines who our parents will be, where we are born, whom we shall meet, fall in love with, have our babies with, and so on. Viewed in this way, the family, place, and culture we find ourselves a part of are the result of karma on a larger scale, a gluey labyrinth or samsaric mandala of interconnections among many individuals.

The collective, be it a family, clan, or larger cultural circle, does not determine but rather reinforces behavior. As beings who seek at the deepest level to eliminate our illusion of separation, we are naturally inclined to socialize, mix and mingle, and create whatever experience of unity we can with those around us. In that process the connections we make, some close and some distant, persist over time, even over lifetimes. In the East the force of this karma is considered so strong as to lead us to be reborn into our own families generation after generation. Blood is, indeed, thicker than water. Likewise, there are some very good reasons the boy next door lives next door.

When one or several beings do anything in any given part of a mandala, it will have an effect on each person within that collective.

Thus it is that Buddhists speak of collective karma. Truly, by karmic law and necessity, we do owe Caesar. But some of us pay more heavily than others, and each of us has our own reaction to the payment.

> *When one or several beings do anything in any given part of a mandala, it will have an effect on each person within that collective. . . . The same thing can happen to many people in a collective for many different reasons.*

There are individual reasons for our connection to any unity. Thus, the same thing can happen to many people in a collective for many different reasons. If an airplane goes down in flames, all the travelers have both individual and shared reasons for being there. If a group experiences racial, religious, or sexual persecution, there are both collective and individual causes.

In the realm of intimacy we therefore cannot discount how the dissolution of our parents' marriage or a history of failed relationships and various family intrigues have an effect on how we view and work with relationships here and now. This is the sort of grist often used in psychotherapy, but the Buddha would say that psychotherapy does not take the analysis far enough. If it's true that we get attracted to our family and parents by force of previous karmic connection born of habitual patterns and their karmic traces, then it follows that we have been lovers, mothers, fathers, sisters, and brothers to one another lifetime after lifetime. We recycle back into our own creation and are given yet another opportunity to work out whatever we need to work out.

Buddhist teaching talks about the unconditional nature of the love our parents show us and the love we should especially show our mothers. Again, with reincarnation not admitted into psychotherapy, we lose a deeper reason for our connection to those who have birthed us, and we lay all the responsibility and blame in their laps. In this way, modern psychoanalytic theory and the therapies it has spawned have done a terrible disservice to the family and our intimate relationships.

Beyond family, larger-scale collective karmas must also impact intimacy issues in our lives. We cannot go unaffected by the fallout from the havoc groups of people have wreaked upon one another over generations. Genocide, slavery, aristocratic prerogative, religious crusades, "ethnic cleansing," indulging in the "spoils of war"—in how many ways have nations or various religious, political, and cultural groups destroyed families, separating husbands from wives and children from parents? The resulting fragmentation and dissolution of entire cultures and ways of life cannot go unpaid for. Someone—perhaps everyone who is remotely connected to any aspect of such violations—must pay in some way.

Many different traditions have their sayings to that effect. They speak of the sins of the father being visited on the son or warn that we should do nothing that could harm the seventh generation. Glibly or with the tongue of a zealot we spout such cultural aphorisms. Yet, how seriously do we look at ourselves as the recipients of the consequences of collective karma? Is it possible that the destruction we have inflicted—however indirectly—upon the sacred bonds of countless lovers in countless cultures over time could be a causal factor in the epidemic of difficult or failed relationships in the modern Western world?

What do we do about collective karma? It is reasonable that we should feel some level of regret and remorse for harmful actions done by those with whom we are loosely or closely associated. At the same time, to indulge in guilt or some form of self-hate campaign does nothing more than create greater negative feeling around us.

Just as we learn methods to become self-aware and to practice living in accordance with our loving nature, we must also develop a social and political awareness that informs the actions we take into the world around us to stop any heinous behavior in our culture. If we are at all interested in developing positive loving relationships we must, by necessity, connect with the altruism that is the inherent social component of our loving nature. We must take social and political action that stands in the way of violations upon others or of anything that our intuition and connection to our loving nature leads us to feel is off the mark. Thus, we begin to cut our bonds to the larger matrix.

> *If we are at all interested in developing positive loving relationships we must, by necessity, connect with the altruism that is the inherent social component of our loving nature.*

We must understand that we cannot love and be in love in an isolated bubble. Such a bubble does not exist anyway, and any we attempt to create will always be pricked by the outside world. Real love that arises from our loving nature is by definition never exclusive; love is always inclusive.

KARMIC GROWTH OPPORTUNITIES

So far we have mostly addressed the harsher realities of karma, whereby we have to contend with the tangled web we have woven—and learn to be a better weaver in the future. But what about the fruition of good deeds that yield good karma? What does good karma look like?

The term *good* is always relative and must be viewed in context based upon perception. For some, a good thing will involve tangible material success and ease in the world—the right job, the right car, the right (beautiful, smart, sexy) mate. For others it may be positive feelings, perhaps also in relation to acquisitions and achievements, or perhaps as just plain great feelings about life in general. For most of us, when our dreams or desires are being fulfilled on some level, the gods must be shining on us. Tradition teaches that we are reaping what seem to be the rewards of the karmic traces of previous lives.

But what if we lose our job, our car is stolen, our Beloved develops an insatiable attraction to someone at work? Is this the exhaustion of good karma? Or is it just bad karma?

Unless we're totally fixated on seeing things in a dualistic, black-and-white reality, determining whether the situation we're facing is bad or good must remain ambiguous. For ambiguity is the signature of relative truth in a relative world. Reality, without a doubt, is what we make it; it looks however it looks based on our own perception and interpretation here and now.

Taking as our example the case of our wayward spouse, we might have any number of reactions. Let's say that rather than become furious, embittered, and closed off in self-pity, choosing to drown it all in bourbon and blame the other for the whole damn mess, we begin to see something the situation reveals to us about ourselves. We see the pressure we placed on our partner and the amount of jealousy we continually displayed whenever he or she even said hello to another. As a result, we soften, become more open and loving, learn to appreciate every aspect of who our Beloved is—even if he or she no longer wants to be with us.

In other words, we have been brought by a seemingly bad situation to a place in our own personal development where we visibly grow as an individual. Our illusions of who we thought our Beloved was and what the rest of our lives together would look like, fueled by desires and dreams, come crashing down around us. The walls we erected around our loving nature, in thinking that it all had to look and feel a certain way, have been reduced to dust. From a wounded, vulnerable space we begin to see more clearly what intimacy is truly about. We have come that much closer to being aware and wholly alive.

If the most noble goal of a relationship is to support and nurture the awakening to our loving nature, then what may have been viewed as a bad thing turns out, from another vantage point, to be a good thing. Such well-learned lessons then become a foundation upon which a more intimate and loving relationship will be built.

Whether bad or good, our karma brings us at any given moment to a crossroads. Whatever the circumstance we find ourselves in, we can succumb to or be swept away by habitual patterns, or we can make efforts to open ourselves up to new possibilities and make the most of whatever life throws at us.

The Tibetans have a saying: "View obstacle as opportunity." The most challenging circumstances, no matter how dire, can provide opportunities for growth. They challenge us to cease being automatons and to embrace our loving nature as a wellspring from which to respond. In fact, I have heard again and again from Tibetan Buddhist teachers that difficult circumstances are more helpful than comfortable or seemingly perfect circumstances in that, being creatures that are "built for pleasure and not for speed," we tend to get lazy and linger in the coziness of what feels good.

> *View obstacle as opportunity. The most challenging circumstances, no matter how dire, can provide opportunities for growth.*

Of course, there are some who feel uncomfortable with their wealth, prosperity, or the seeming ease of their life. Based on such feelings, they may choose to place themselves in dangerous or dire circumstances. But in the end the inauthenticity of such choices becomes increasingly obvious. Adversity as a style never wears well. Life is challenging enough without putting ourselves in situations that will, more than likely, bring out the worst in us. Without much effort, even as we try to do the best we can, there will be plenty of challenges that naturally arise. We really don't have to go out looking for them.

Trusting our loving nature as much as we can in the moment, based on the karmic traces that have brought us to this point, we make our decisions and act, setting in motion a cascade of events that will demand our participation. Whether we participate willingly or not, there will always be a piper to play. And the tune being played will sound ever so familiar. In the moment, when we hear the melody, we can embellish its beauty and erase the dissonant chords. Karma provides the music. How we dance to it is entirely up to us.

Knowing that this is one of the most challenging and defining tasks we are called to embark upon, all of the world's wisdom traditions seek in their own way to offer methods and techniques that help us to open up to the moment; to "be here now"; to sever the ties that bind and create strands of goodness that connect us heart to heart in the ocean of limitless love.

This is the primary purpose of the meditative methods taught by the Buddha. As we develop the awareness and resourcefulness to cut through the habitual patterns that tie us to the karmic traces of our own creation, it becomes effortless to live out of and create in a space of love. To be in a place or frame of mind where we open to such wisdom teachings and methods is considered fortunate karma. We become fortunate as we learn to transform bad into good, obstacle into opportunity, and good into something greater that gloriously embraces and nurtures others.

To be in a relationship in which our partner wishes to develop a similar awareness and resourcefulness and to stand beside us as we do the same is doubly fortunate.

Part Three

Sex and
Sexual Matters

Sexuality and Spirituality: A Buddhist Perspective

The Lotus-flower, the sex organ of the partner,
is an ocean filled with Bliss. This Lotus-flower
is also a transparent place, where the Thought
of Enlightenment can rise up. When it is
united with the Scepter, the male organ, their
mixture is compared to the Elixir produced
from the combination of myrrh and nutmeg.
From their union a pure knowledge arises,
which explains the nature of things.
—KALACHAKRA TANTRA (EXCERPTED IN *SEXUAL SECRETS,*
BY DOUGLAS AND SLINGER, P. 246)

Being as we are in the Realm of Desire, the Buddha was well aware of sexual attraction and the potential within sexuality. Therefore, to banish it from being a playful, dynamic aspect of our loving nature would have denied the humanity of those who sought his guidance. We see the results of such repression when cultures embrace puritanical or fundamentalist approaches to life and spirituality. Historical and current examples of this include the tradition of temple eunichs, the burning of inspiring ladies as witches, and the stoning of women in public if a part of a shoulder or thigh is exposed.

Of course, the most commonly marketed portrayal of Buddhism in the West is a vision of monks and nuns in flowing saffron or maroon robes. These images conjure notions of piety, purity, and celibacy, giving Buddhism an aura and reputation of being lofty, otherworldly, and certainly nothing that could possibly be practiced by the average man or woman on the street. Normal people who do practice it must be involved in a lesser version, somehow watered down for those of less noble virtue. This view probably arises from the sacred versus mundane controversy inherent in the more commonly practiced Judeo-Christian traditions, coupled with a definite lack of historical insight on the Buddhist traditions throughout the ages.

It is also a simple fact that most of the better-known or popular Buddhist teachers writing and teaching at this time are indeed celibate. Virtually none of them has been or remains in a committed, intimate relationship, yet they have a remarkable ability to understand the human condition in all its many layers of life experience, including intimate relationships. Perhaps it is because the reasons for celibacy in Buddhist orders have more to do with esoteric spiritual disciplines than some exoteric display of virtue. Certainly there is this dimension. Yet, there remains a more relaxed, worldly dimension in understanding celibacy's usefulness. With respect to Tantric sexuality, some of these teachers may have experience in this area. But for the most part, while one may be able to engage a teacher in a discussion of how to work with or channel sexual energy for meditational purposes, rarely will you find a teacher writing or speaking about sexual intimacy in explicit terms. There are three main Tibetan Buddhist sects (Nyingma, Kagyu, and Sakya) that have lay or nonmonastic teachers who may be married or in relationship. Monastic or not, we all know that there is more to relationships than sex. And thus, because Buddhist training helps one to understand the nature and dynamics of the mind, all of these teachers can competently guide us through the labryinth of relationships.

The Buddha was not a prude, but he was not a hedonist either. He wasn't moralistic, but neither was he a nihilist. When looking at the above-cited sexually explicit quote from the Kalachakra Tantra, one wonders if perhaps the Buddha was just speaking theoretically or metaphorically, as the words seem uncharacteristic of what most of us think of when we think of the Buddha's teaching. The Kalachakra Tantra was the teaching the Buddha gave to the beings of Shambhala, a realm that is said to exist even to this day. In Shambhala, the Buddha found a society enlightened at every level, where spirit was seen and mindfulness practiced in all facets of life, including sexual expressiveness. It is said that the Buddha in his incarnation as Kalachakra gave the most profound teachings of his dharma.

Yet the Buddha knew that for many the idea of tempering the heat and working with the energies of sexual intimacy was beyond their capacity to see this energy in anything but a lustful way. He saw then the need to encourage temperance and celibacy for some, while sharing teachings and practices with others who were ready and willing to utilize sexual energy for a more full-bodied spiritual expressiveness. Thus along with the monks and nuns who followed a celibate way of life, there arose a class of noncelibate yogis and tantrikas—the mahasiddhas—who were every bit as devoted to the teachings of the Buddha as were the monastics.

Some may think that creating this division was the Buddha's way of compromising—an attempt to rein in both groups of people who wanted to hear what he had to share. Others think that this is an indication that Buddhism encourages its own form of libertinism. Some modern and quite serious students of Buddhism think of these two groups as the fun-loving Buddhists (the yogis, siddhas, and tantrikas) and the boring ones (the monastics). All these views are simplistic and completely false. For in truth, the capacities and understandings of the lay and noncelibate paths are predicated on developing an understanding that comes from the monastic traditions of the Hinayana and Mahayana. The morality, ethics, and ecological sensibility of these two perspectives is the firm foundation from which one can then expand one's awareness and activity to include every aspect of life.

THE CELIBATE PATH

I am sometimes asked whether this vow of celibacy is really desirable and indeed whether it is really possible. Suffice to say that its practice is not simply a matter of suppressing sexual desires. On the contrary, it is necessary to fully accept the existence of these desires and transcend them by the power of reasoning. . . . Thus as Nagarjuna said, "When you have an itch, you scratch. But not to itch at all is better than any amount of scratching."
—His Holiness the Dalai Lama, *The Dalai Lama's Book of Daily Meditations* (p. 163)

While it may seem unlikely that celibacy should have any impact at all on the sexual relations of anyone but the person following that particular lifestyle, celibacy has had and continues to have a profound influence on all relationships in society. Much of what we are taught with respect to morals, ethics, and sexuality is done by spiritual teachers who follow a celibate path. Likewise, how these spiritual teachers handle and come to terms with their own sexuality and sexual expression through the path of celibacy has a profound impact on us. Their teachings and examples follow us right into the bedroom. It is, therefore, important to look at the role of celibacy in our society today and its overall connection to spirituality and sexual relationships—the human experience of the spiritual being.

If we recall the account of the Buddha's life in chapter 1, the strictest monastic traditions are a part of the Hinayana tradition. These are especially useful for men and women who find themselves caught up in the suffering they experience from strong attachments. Giving up a worldly life and choosing one of simplicity and celibacy, they begin to lessen this attachment.

The rules and regulations of the Hinayana monastic traditions are designed to help people keep their vows. For example, monks are not allowed to touch women—not even to shake hands. Nor do nuns touch men. In fact, the rules and regulations for nuns are stricter than those for monks. One may think that this is a clear example of male chauvinism on the part of the Buddha. However, it is the antithesis of that.

In a workshop where this issue was brought up, the Venerable Khenpo Karthar Rinpoche explained that the more rigorous regulations as to where and when nuns could be seen and how they should behave, especially around men, is in no way related to women's inferiority. In fact, they are seen as generally more disciplined than monks. Monks—and men in general—have greater tendencies to bend the rules and may try to tempt, taunt, or otherwise engage the nuns. Thus, the greater restrictions on nuns are for their protection. In this matter, men are definitely the weaker sex.

The Mahayana traditions also have monastics who live by similar rules, but their involvement in the community involves different standards. As they are working less on attachment and more on strengthening compassion, the taboos against touch are less important. Especially in the case of Tibetan monks and nun, it is commonly thought here in the West that we must be on our best behavior around such "holy" people. In truth, aside from there being a less restrictive attitude around physical contact in the Mahayana, Tibetans are a very "touchy-feely" people. Thus, these monks and nuns often feel touch deprived in the West upon the pedestals where we place them.

Celibacy is not a principle or practice Westerners have an easy time with. In the East, celibacy is intended to serve as a means toward spiritual unfoldment. The skillful suppression of sexual urges redirects energies in the body that can facilitate the development of new levels of insight and compassion for all beings with no regard to their sex.

This does not mean all monks or nuns throughout the ages, including today, have had this level of mastery of their sexual urges. In analyzing Gedun Chöpel's "Treatise on Passion," scholar Jeffrey Hopkins notes that homosexual acts were not an uncommon phenomenon in Tibetan monasteries of the past,[1] although in modern times I am unaware of any reporting of such incidents. It must be remembered that many boys and girls were and still are sent to monasteries at a very early age. Sometimes this has occurred in families with too many children to raise, when the financial burden of them all has been unmanageable. Other times, the child sent away has been weak, unattractive, or deformed. Families have also long considered it good karma for one of their sons to become a monk. Therefore, family expectations have been placed on certain children to honor the family in this way. With such expectations and customs, there's no certainty that novice monks or nuns would have purely religious intentions, let alone a liking for their cloistered environment. When certain monks or nuns have clearly been struggling to maintain their vows of celibacy, a skillful abbot or abbess has encouraged them to give up their vows, go out and get married, and have children. Then perhaps later on in life they could rejoin their order.

For some orders of robed practitioners, including Tibetan lamas and even lay practitioners, celibacy is encouraged during certain periods of meditation or in spiritual retreat settings in order for those involved to redirect their focus and energy. Once the practice or retreat is complete, the vow of celibacy comes to an end. In Thailand where Hinayana is the predominant form of Buddhism, it is customary for eldest sons to shave their heads and take vows of celibacy for forty-nine days following the death of a parent. This is in keeping with the teachings from *The Tibetan Book of the Dead*. Having his or her child live a "pure" religious life during this time is considered beneficial to the future karma of the parent who has died. It is also a Thai belief that we get reborn into our own families. Thus, after forty-nine days, the eldest son would complete his vows, go back to his wife, and hopefully conceive his own mother or father.

Within Western cultures, and religious circles in particular, the practice of celibacy, for the most part, has been viewed as an external demonstration of commitment to religious life and of the primacy and exclusivity of a relationship to God. In some sense, even though there are words sanctifying carnal expression between husband and wife, being celibate or, in more lay terms, being chaste, is culturally touted as the quintessential expression of devotion to God and the spiritual life. With the inner or energetic significance being largely lost, the outer meaning of celibacy has taken on disproportionate importance, creating a rigid, repressive form of celibacy that has proven disastrous in recent years; more than likely, it has wreaked havoc on the religious landscape for longer than most are prepared to admit. When pleasure is blended inextricably with sin and guilt, imbalanced and often forced sexual acts follow that perpetuate low self-esteem for both perpetrator and victim. This is merely the cloistered version of the schizophrenic relationship our entire culture has with sexuality. The separation of sexuality from religious life or spirituality may in fact be one of the causes for the cultural warping of sex. Carnal desire becomes a reminder of our lowly state, something we should strive to rise above. In puritan, orthodox, and fundamentalist circles, sex becomes hallowed only in the context of marriage. Lip service may be paid to the joys of sexuality, but the greater emphasis is on procreation—the so-called highest form of sexuality. Consequently, contraception becomes the enemy of this sacred expression, and thus an enemy of religion. We can enjoy ourselves and enjoy our spouse if we're making love and leaving open—or better still, actively wanting—the possibility of procreation. With that door closed, we are only indulging in our base nature. Worst yet is that contraception makes sex available to even the unbetrothed. Abstinence supported by guilt and fear of damnation becomes the secular celibacy of the young and restless, the unwed, and the uninitiated.

From such a dualistic perspective, celibacy becomes an icon, a symbol of humankind's triumph over itself. It serves no purpose but to taint joyful feelings with remorse and confine our urges to the shadow side of our being. Ultimately, this sort of repression—since it has nothing to do with the channeling of the sexual energy—only becomes an excruciating exercise in self-denial and breeds obsession with what is being denied. Penises and breasts become deified. We become titillated by licentious, inappropriate behavior and acts, and eventually this perversion finds its way into our arts and media. In our contemporary culture, this phenomenon is all-pervasive: consider the endless sexual references and innuendos for nearly every age group of TV watchers, the vast empire of pornography on the Internet, the obvious pelvic thrusting of barely clad cheerleaders during sporting events. Playing to our unfilled, repressed desires has become the greatest marketing tool. If we get the right car, do we get the leggy lady in black leather or the dark handsome stranger who was sitting in it on the billboard? On a rational level, we know this isn't true. But anything that has been pushed into the shadows does not concern itself with rationality.

Even more alarming is the way that sexual expression and violence are intertwined—in rape, incest, adultery, and various forms of sadism. We watch what is illicit, licentious, dangerous. Desire and passion get pushed into the realms of lust and obsession. Whether we are willing to admit to it or not, such rigid, unhealthy images and views make their way into our beds, creating a context for unhelpful fantasies, manipulative behavior, and disappointment. I do not look to media as the cause for such problems, but rather to religions that have lost their connection to the spiritual being having a human experience. Such religious and cultural schizophrenia around sexuality has also had an impact on Buddhism and other Eastern religions with celibate traditions that are practiced in the West. While celibacy and large groups of celibates are quite common to encounter in the East, it is not so here in the West. Thus, the experience and expectations around such people are not always clearly understood. Because we are unfamiliar with the ranks and delineations within these spiritual communities, there are also some who wrongly make the assumption that all spiritual practitioners are celibate. This has been the cause of embarrassing moments as well as the occasional scandal. While there may be rogues among the many excellent spiritual teachers, there also are both men and women who abdicate their common sense or personal responsibility when in the presence of those whom they hold in deference, resulting in great confusion about the role of celibacy as it relates to spiritual followers. Whether these sexual encounters are mutual and respectful or inappropriate and harmful is the sole responsibility of the teacher.

THE NONCELIBATE PATH

The use of sexuality and actual sexual expression as a means of teaching, transformation, and transmission between teacher and student exists in the Vajrayana or Tantric schools of Mahayana Buddhism. When two people are engaged in Tantric sexual union, the blocks to deeper compassion and insight are transformed. Wisdom (the feminine) informs skillful means (the masculine). Sacred sexuality or sexuality as a pathway to spiritual fulfillment is a radical notion in the West, but in the chapter that follows we will look at the practices of Tantric sexuality and what it can contribute to individual transformation, greater levels of intimacy and beauty between friends and partners, and the path to enlightenment. There is certainly no need to engage in Tantric sexual practices in order to practice Tantra in Buddhism. Likewise the model of teachers and consorts is not the norm. But, if such practices and possibilities were altogether dismissed, the juiciness and dynamism of this level of Buddhism and what it can contribute to individual transformation, greater levels of intimacy and beauty between friends and partners, and the path to enlightenment would be severely compromised. A soft spirituality that runs into the same dualistic conundrums as any other Western religion would remain to bore us all. The spiritual world would become a far more pastel place than many of us would care to live in.

8

Healthy Sex, Healthy Body, Healthy Spirit

A sexual relationship may be an act of deep communion between body and spirit. . . . When we are approached casually or carelessly, with an attitude that is less than tender, we feel insulted in our body and soul. Someone who approaches us with respect, tenderness, and utmost care is offering us deep communication, deep communion.
—Thich Nhat Hanh, *Teachings on Love* (p. 89)

In "The Treatise on Passion"—what could be considered the Tibetan contribution to the world's books on eroticism—Gedun Chöpel, a rather controversial figure in modern Tibetan culture, makes the key point that the most important aspect in healthy sexual relationships is mutuality.[1] Chöpel is referring to that moment when each of us comes to the acts of physical loving seeing the other as our equal. Throughout his descriptions of foreplay and various sexual acts, he always emphasizes that what the man does should please the woman and what the woman does should please the man. (A discussion of homosexual love was not a part of his text, but it will be discussed in chapter 9.)

Generosity and compassion, outward expressions of our loving nature, are fundamental ingredients of positive, healthy, joyful sex. This doesn't mean that we should not enjoy the pleasure we feel with our partner. We need to steer between self-indulgence (just "getting off" for its own sake) and duty (so aptly spoken of in British society as "doing it for queen and country"), extremes that do not connect us to our loving nature and often lead to greater self-absorption or denial. Between these extremes is the possibility of a loving embrace that is open, sweet, and fresh—containing all the ingredients of tenderness. The desire to please our lover is what gives the experience its openness. Its sweetness comes from our lover's willingness to reciprocate in kind. And the experience of freshness is where the personal boundaries that seemingly separate us dissolve.

> *The desire to please our lover is what gives the sexual experience its openness. Its sweetness comes from our lover's willingness to reciprocate in kind. And the experience of freshness is where the personal boundaries that seemingly separate us dissolve.*

LOVE ESSENTIALS

Whether we look at sex from the most carnal or most spiritual perspective, mutuality is always essential. At the same time, in the act of making love, different levels of experience can arise. The Venerable Chögyam Trungpa Rinpoche once commented that our sexual organs are organs of communication. The act of communication includes what we transmit, what the other receives and perceives from what we have transmitted, a response on his or her part, our reception of that response, and how both of us surmise what the whole gestalt means—a full self-reflecting feedback loop. Sex, like any other act of communication, can be experienced and interpreted in a variety of ways. And there is no guarantee that what we get out of the moment is what our partner gets out of that same moment.

Looking at sexual intimacy from the point of view of the body-speech-mind trinity of Buddhist thought, the first level of experience we can have is in the body—making love with a sense of sheer physical power and worldly joy. This is the truly carnal experience—earthy and warm and solid physical contact at its best. Lovemaking at this level provides grounding, putting us back in our bodies as a relatively reliable reference point. This experience should not be dismissed or demeaned. In our fast-paced, overly stimulating modern world, it is a relief and a comfort to feel anything so viscerally and to reconnect in that way with our humanity. We are then able to look around and reconnect with the world of beings around us. Most important, we are reminded of our connection with and the support we receive from our Beloved.

Even in the Tibetan medical texts, which originate from the teachings of another enlightened being who is known as the Healing or Medicine Buddha, the benefits of sexual intercourse at this level are acknowledged. Author Terry Clifford, in her *Tibetan Buddhist Medicine and Psychiatry*, notes that for some psychiatric conditions of women and men, frequent sexual intercourse is prescribed. In these cases, sex has less to do with emotional bonding and more to do with reconnecting to the physical as a way of bringing a person to his or her senses, figuratively and literally.[2] I am reminded of a crude but honest scene in the movie *L.A. Story*, in which a female character, having just flown to Los Angeles from London, comments that she is not feeling anything that a "fuck and a good night's sleep" won't cure. Anyone who has experienced jet lag can appreciate the sanity of her prescription.

In the speech part of the trinity, we are looking at interaction, what is transpiring between two individuals at the emotionally expressive level. Here, intentions, needs, and wants can vary considerably, and the dance between two people can cover a full range of emotions. Sometimes we come to bed full of ourselves, wanting to express our energy. Other times we are unsure and seek comfort. Sometimes we're feeling trapped inside ourselves and need to reach out. Sometimes we just feel silly and want to romp around. These and other variations can also occur in many combinations. And what our partner comes to bed with as wants or needs may be similar or different. One may want to tango while the other wants to slow-dance.

In the end, our experience at this level is satisfying when, regardless of where we're coming from, we are treated with mutuality and have a sense that our partner is present and willing to go through whatever dance we need to go through in order to feel more space and joy. If both partners are willing to oblige each other, even if the needs are very different, a dance that is a fusion of needs and wants can bring satisfaction and joy to both. By acknowledging and bowing to each other's loving nature, we create a new dance that is an expression of the moment, perfect and honest. Again, neither compromise nor abdication is necessary.

It bears mentioning that two lovers won't necessarily come to a similar point in their experience of this perfection. Both may not want, after making love, to gaze into each other's eyes and cuddle up. People's expressions at physical and emotional levels are conveyed in a variety of ways, based on individual history plus what Tibetan medicine identifies as different body-mind types. Our partner may smile and bubble while we lie content and pensive. One of us may want to talk and share. The other may want to go within.

Remember that as beings of desire in a social reality, we tend to create stereotypes, or frozen images, of who we are, who we are supposed to be in relation to various others, and who those others should be in relation to us. It only stands to reason that in the most intimate form of communication, where risk and vulnerability are most evident, expectations are high and every gesture and nuance take on magnified significance. Judgment and unnecessary critical commentary in such tender times can truly spoil a beautiful moment.

If we want to step around or cut through the potential or actual dramas that arise in lovemaking, we need ways in which we can catch ourselves watching, assuming, inferring, and judging. We need to be able to breathe in, breathe out, let go, and open up. Here, too, the benefits of meditation practice come in handy. Using the teachings of Zen patriarch Sengstan on letting go of preferences and opinions (see chapter 5) can also remind us to be less judgmental of ourselves and to open to our partner's needs, wants, and style of communication. In trusting our loving nature, we allow ourselves to experience a rainbow of new and subtle experiences in intimate expression. An exquisite tenderness then arises that is both humbling and exhilarating.

> *In trusting our loving nature, we allow ourselves to experience a rainbow of new and subtle experiences in intimate expression. An exquisite tenderness then arises that is both humbling and exhilarating.*

The third level of experience, that of the mind or spirit, is where sexual embrace acts as a catalyst for transformation at the deepest level of our being. Beyond being a physically exquisite event that is emotionally joyful, it actually creates a shift that occurs within us and makes us see our world differently. In the long run, this is the most significant gift two partners can offer each other. For long after the visual and visceral memories of great sex fade away, what will be left are the ways in which our passions brought us to deeper insights, compassion, and connection. One sees this phenomenon in the knowing glances of elderly couples who still show a playful love for each other even though the heat of passion at the physical level has long since faded.

TANTRA AND TANTRIC SEXUALITY

It should be understood that all three levels, the physical, emotional, and spiritual, happen simultaneously. As in all experiences in life, what we get out of what we're doing depends on where we're starting from. Sometimes we need physical contact and sometimes emotional expression or support; at other times we are able to abandon ourselves and experience something at a deeper level. Furthermore, our partner may start from a very different place and arrive at a place that is distinctly different from the one we get to.

In truth, sex is a high form of communication with many subtleties. How we get to where we consummate the moment, what is meant and experienced in the act of consummation, and all the aftereffects that follow create the ground and texture for further transactions. It is for these reasons that mindfulness with sexual expression is so important.

Bringing mindfulness into the discussion of sexual expression inevitably leads us to what many consider the highest form of sexual expression—Tantra.

When studying Eastern traditions, Hindu and Buddhist, we hear of Tantra and Tantric love. Indeed, this is the highest form of loving sexual embrace; lovemaking in this context is grounding, joyful, spontaneous, and transformative. Tantric sex has made its way into the marketplace because spirituality combined with sexuality is something that intrigues many Westerners. But few people comprehend what Tantric sexuality is really about or know what is needed on the part of its practitioners even prior to engaging in the physical acts involved.

Thus, it is highly questionable whether the successful marketing of such a high practice yields the results and benefits that it is intended to produce.

Undeniably, a Tantric weekend workshop that teaches new positions and ways of manipulating sexual energy and power can indeed transform habitual patterns and bring a freshness back into a faltering relationship. It can also produce deluded people with elitist attitudes who believe they have now become Tantric studs or consorts. Worse, a raising of expectations and preferences can result to a degree that the freshness of relating in the moment is destroyed. When lofty goals are not met, people are left with a deep disappointment. This disappointment can be so powerful that it has the potential to ruin their long-term relationships or cause them to rule out relating to people they may have otherwise found attractive or interesting.

What exactly is meant by the term *Tantra?*

Tantra is commonly thought to be synonymous with *sex*. Just type *Tantra* into a search engine on the Internet and watch what pops up.

Contrary to popular view, Tantric practice is not primarily about sexual practices with a partner. In fact, the proper Tantric perspective is that men have their female side and women have their male side; both possess the energetics of the opposite sex. That a man is more identified with outward expression and action in the world—skillful means—is expressed in his form, physique, sexual attributes, and the tendencies that we associate with men. That a woman is more identified with inner expression and unconditional love—wisdom—is expressed in her form, physique, sexual attributes, and female tendencies.

Tantra in the Buddhist tradition means *continuity* or *lineage*. The transmission and teachings from an enlightened being, a Buddha, get passed on in an unbroken line to worthy students who, in turn, become the teachers of future students, and so on. In Tantric spiritual disciplines, a student engages in spiritual practices in which the energetic form of the original enlightened being—the source of the transmissions and teachings—is invoked, meditated upon, and identified with. This form is called a *yidam*, which has as one of its meanings "river back to the source."

Although a tantrika—one who studies Tantra—may feel an affinity for a particular enlightened being he or she would wish to emulate, the selection of yidam is usually based on the recommendation of the tantrika's teacher. To come to full realization on this path, the tantrika must maintain an altruistic outlook and commit to doing whatever the teacher lays out for him or her as the practice and methods necessary to reach that same enlightenment expression. Tantra, therefore, is a path of direct identification. Practitioners develop the mental and physical capacities, the proper view, and the compassion to engage in what is considered the most direct and challenging path to enlightenment.

When uninformed viewers of Tantric art see a male and female form embracing, they think that this is the Buddhist version of an education in sexual positions—postcards from the *Kama Sutra*, perhaps the most well known and frequently cited treatise on erotic love, from India. In fact what these *thangkas*, or sacred paintings, are really trying to convey is the integration of the male and female archetypes and their energies within each practitioner. That is, in order for a male tantrika to attain full realization, to become a completely whole and living example of enlightenment, he needs to access and fully integrate into his being his female side—the wisdom that is the she-archetype within him. Skillful means is then tempered with a deeper appreciation of Emptiness (so the practitioner won't be so "cocky"), leading to a profound compassion. In order for a female tantrika to manifest her full enlightenment, she must access and fully integrate into her way of being the he-archetype within her. Wisdom becomes dynamic and able to transform the world around her as skillful means provides the female practitioner with power, courage, and savvy.

To accomplish such internal feats, tantrikas see the body as possessing a network of subtle channels, essences, and winds. These are integrally connected to what are commonly known as the chakras. By visualizing their bodies in this way, seeing the deities and lotus petals associated with the chakras in their bodies, and moving the winds in a specific manner throughout their physical beings as described in their particular Tantric practice, they undergo a deep psychic transformation that begins to inform and in turn transform denser layers of their emotional and physical beings.

Are these constructs real? Are we truly these networks filled with lotus flowers and gods and goddesses? When asked this question at a conference in Boulder, Colorado, in the late 1980s, His Holiness the Dalai Lama explained that this was not literally the case, but that it was useful to view the body this way.

As beings in the Realm of Desire, we are strongly connected to our senses. Thus, we can indeed create change by altering our perceptions; seeing energy moving inside us as various colors and lights that activate deities with various attributes; visualizing in our mind's eye that our body and the world around us are a mandala of energy and light; and using sounds (mantras) that are intended to activate within us the qualities and attributes of the being we seek to identify with and emulate. Consequently, it doesn't matter whether what we're doing is real or fictional. If it does what it's supposed to do, that's all that matters.

These Tantric practices are generally done on our own. That is, a person will receive the transmission and teachings and then go off to practice until realization is achieved. Thus, such practices are done in both lay and monastic settings. Tantrikas can appear as monks or nuns or anyone else.

It is also interesting to note that within the context of the meditations and realizations within the experience of enlightenment in the tantric tradition, very graphic sexual language is often chosen. The words in the following verses of the "Mystic Song" of the mahasiddha Saraha are not intended to titillate as much as they are to convey in dynamic terms how one should approach such a path.

> *High is the mountain of the spinal column, and at*
> *the top of it, there sits the Bliss-bestowing girl in the*

*form of a huntress. She is all covered with peacock
feathers and a beautiful garland of flowers is around
her gazelle-like neck.*

*"O exalted hunter! Mad hunter!" So exclaims the
girl on the mountain peak. "I am your dearest
mistress; my name is Spontaneous Wave of Bliss."*

*Many are the trees on the mountain. The hunter-girl,
decked with beautiful earrings of lightning and
thunder, plays alone in the forest. The bedstead of
the Three Essentials of Body, Speech, and Mind is
made ready. In expectant Bliss, the hunter spreads
the bedclothes. Then the serpent-like hunter and the
selfless goddess pass their night of love on that bed.*

—"Mystic Song" of the great mahasiddha Saraha,
Sexual Secrets, by Douglas and Slinger (p. 241)

Although we have been pointing to the metaphorical and symbolic
aspects of Tibetan iconography and Tantric literature, I must remind
the reader of the quote cited from the Kalachakra Tantra. The enlightened view of sexuality as depicted in this quote is real Tantric sexual
practice. Thus "dual" Tantric practices do exist, whereby male and
female tantrikas join in full sexual embrace. The purpose of dual Tantra
is to magnify the intensity and quicken the transformational process by
creating a psychic circuitry between the two involved. This is done
through touch, penetration, visualization, and, above all, intention.

As prerequisites to Tantric lovemaking, mutuality and an affec-
tionate loving bond between the partners are essential. From the Buddhist point of view, working with subtle energies in the body must be
rooted in a morality that demonstrates a caring and regard for all
beings, especially our partner. We see the Buddhanature in all and,
therefore, make no attempt to seek power over or manipulate another for our own sense of glory and realization. The sacred biographi-

cal stories of the yogis and mahasiddhas of India and Tibet demonstrate that they had great respect and regard for their consorts. These consorts were great beings themselves, sometimes even more advanced in their own spiritual realization.

This is a critical point. The Venerable Khenpo Karthar Rinpoche has said that a male tantrika's greatest violation to the Tantric law or view is to denigrate a woman. Danish lama Ole Nydahl once commented to me that he had met very few men who claimed to be doing Tantra who didn't seem to be somewhat macho and callous toward their partners or women in general. Women are wisdom personified. Without wisdom, the male aspect of skillful means lacks compassion. Without wisdom, there is no enlightenment. For a man to abuse a woman demeans and degrades what he needs most.

One of the classic Tantric embraces depicted in Tibetan iconography involves the man sitting in a cross-legged posture and the woman straddling his waist with her legs wrapped around him. In this manner she settles onto his lap and penis until there is full, deep vaginal penetration.

Penetration is performed unprotected. Contraception is not considered relevant, as a tantrika is supposed to retain all seminal fluid. The use of condoms, coils, diaphragms, foams, and even oral contraception interferes with visceral stimulation and the healthy unimpeded flow of subtle energy and impulse. The couple is kissing in an open-mouthed, French-kiss style, with the tips of their tongues touching. This oral connection actually creates a tingling sensation in the genitals.

Sitting in this manner, the partners remain relatively still and focused. As the male breathes in, he imagines that at the tip of his penis he is drawing in the wisdom energy of the female, as if his penis were a straw. This energy then circulates up the spine in the form of red light, passes under the skull over the head, and comes to a point just below the nose. As he breathes out, he visualizes the energy as turning white and being passed to his partner through the tip of his tongue. From her tongue it travels down the front of her body until it comes to the clitoris.

Their breath is coordinated so that as the man breathes out, the woman is breathing in, and vice versa. If during this ritual the male's penis begins to go soft, the female tantrika draws up her vaginal muscles to reengorge his penis with blood.

As the energy builds between them, there may arise the desire to indulge in full fluid orgasm—to ejaculate, something that both men and women do. Tantra teaches that in the seminal fluid of both genders, there are drops of vital energy—*tigle* in Tibetan—the spending of which ages the body more quickly and leads to a dulling of the senses. To avoid this release, male tantrikas are encouraged to draw up their anus and groin and females, their pelvic floor muscles, thus redirecting those feelings through the entire body all the way to the top of the head. The result is a full body orgasm—an event of exquisite and indescribable bliss.

If this drawing-up doesn't transform the urge to ejaculate, it is considered harmful to the body to repress that urge. In other words, let it out! Those who elect to withdraw before ejaculation should try to do it slowly and mindfully. Fast withdrawal can be a shock, but may be necessary—especially when there is a strong apprehension about conceiving. Those who elect to share seminal fluid must be in a frame of mind to do so joyfully, with full awareness of the possible consequences of their actions. The act of sharing seminal fluid presupposes that one is willing to risk the possibility of pregnancy with one's partner and that one is knowledgeable of the sexual healthiness of one's partner. In an age of AIDS and other sexually transmitted diseases, to think of performing such an act without this knowledge is clearly not advised.

What is described here is in no way the full palette of what is included in Tantric sexuality. There are variations in positions, methods of stimulation, and ways in which energies are circulated. My main point in discussing Tantric practices is to draw attention to the level of attention and mutual love that is demanded in the practice of dual Tantra. This sort of Tantric sex—pure, unadulterated, compassionate, and loving—truly leads to spiritual transformation. Performed with the right intention and compassion, Tantric practices create a bond between partners that transcends any conventional definitions of love and partnership. More important, the good feelings and power created from these practices become visible in the words and deeds of the tantrikas, in their growing wisdom and ever more unconditional love.

Because of the power and demands of Tantric sex, it is important to engage in an exploration of dual Tantra under the right conditions, with the proper motive, frame of mind, and physical capabilities. Beware of any seminar or crash course promising to make you a Tantric lover in one weekend. These claims undervalue the power and significance of what Tantra is promoting. My general advice is to seek out teachers who are connected to or come with the recommendation from a recognized Tantric lineage. Information about such lineages and teachers can be found in some of the books listed in the bibliography. When you meet such teachers, be bold enough to ask them if they teach dual Tantra. Then be prepared for whatever response is given. Some may know it and will be willing to teach. Some may know it and will say they don't, either because they really don't, they don't teach it, or they don't think you are ready to learn. You will find that to embark on the path of dual Tantra requires intelligence, persistence, daring, and, most of all, the desire to express fully and fearlessly your loving nature with your Beloved. Without this last prerequisite, one is only performing sexual gymnastics. With it, you can prepare yourself for a lifetime adventure.

MORALITY AND PROMISCUITY

Tantric Buddhist literature is explicit in its transmission, instructions, and commentary on dual Tantra. Beyond this, discussion and recommendations in Tantric texts and Buddhist texts from all traditions focus on sexual morality as important precepts to live by. The rules or principles mentioned are not meant to be dogmatic or to force people into some kind of stiff mold. Rather, they are based on a profound appreciation of what it takes to create harmonious couples, families, and communities. Their logic stems from a deep understanding of who we are biologically, emotionally, and spiritually.

For the most part, the spiritual texts speak of sexual morality in terms of mutuality and respect. Above all in Buddhism comes attitude. Not treating all people with equanimity, not honoring the Buddhanature of others, denigrating them, seducing them to suit our own sexual whims, and otherwise taking advantage of others, as in rape or incest—all such behaviors are unacceptable.

Because these admonitions come in spiritual texts, we are first and foremost advised not to treat members of religious orders in this manner, including all spiritual teachers and especially people who have taken vows of celibacy. The texts then go on to warn against adultery, whereby vows people have made to each other are violated—vows that may be more conditional and worldly perhaps, but probably as important to those who make them in true faith as the vows made by those vowing to the religious orders they serve.

There is a logic to viewing and protecting such vows as sacred. Most cultures and societies consider them to have a stabilizing effect. Therefore, going into deeper whys and wherefores may seem unnecessary or irrelevant. However, in destabilized societies where cultural rules are blended, blurred, obliterated, or rapidly changing, admonitions and threats of hellfire and damnation or karmic fallout seem to carry less weight. The tyranny of freedom, once again, raises its nasty head, and we are confronted with needing to make personal decisions in a Realm of Desire out of control.

Beyond monks, nuns, and other people's husbands, wives, or mates, Tantric medical texts—the teachings of the Medicine Buddha—go even further in specifying that no one should have sexual relations with animals, dishonorable persons, pregnant or menstruating women, and women with weakening conditions. The inclusion of these categories demonstrates an understanding of medical and energetic realities as an important foundation for Buddhist morality.

It should be obvious from our discussion of dual Tantra that sexual intercourse and the energy that it creates and sets in motion for individuals and between partners is extremely powerful. It can be ultimately transformative, as it is in the fruition of dual Tantra practice. But even for those whose intent is not Tantric, sexual intercourse in itself can be life changing. Losing one's virginity is a profound event.

Even done with mixed intentions, with contraception involved, or with no motivation beyond feeling good, intercourse creates what it does because of the way it moves energy in the subtle channels of the body. According to Tantric tradition, it is this stimulation that affects our nerves and senses, influencing our physical and emotional bodies. Deep psychic impressions are created that will leave us with an etheric connection to whomever we share this act with.

What follows is a deeper exploration of the categories listed above denoting those with whom, according to Buddhist texts, sexual relations should be avoided.

Members of Religious Orders

In doing their spiritual work, monks and nuns—who, for the most part, have taken vows because of their strong attachments—are trying to cool out their desires. Part of their commitment is to suppress and rechannel their sexual desires in particular. When they are seduced into sexual passion and intercourse, the subtle channels of their bodies are stimulated, leaving strong impressions with them that may take much time and effort to redirect.

I have noted that Western monks and nuns in particular tend to have histories of having been incested or raped; in some cases, they were extremely promiscuous before they took robes. Thus, much of their work requires rechanneling the impressions they are left with or the desires that are their tendencies. In most cases, I have witnessed a repression or denial that makes their celibacy an escape and their monastic life a place where they can hide out to avoid confronting such issues. No doubt this is a reality for monks and nuns from every quarter of the world.

I am reminded of a Chinese monk with whom my wife and I were very close. He told us that he went into retreat for ten years in the mountains because of "women trouble." Not so surprisingly, when he came out of retreat, the abbot from his order assigned him to run a nunnery in the West. He managed to keep this position for two years before he requested to be released from it. When we met him, he was living in the woods and getting by with his Chinese medical skills. Again, not so surprisingly, he found that the only people who came to see him for treatment were women with gynecological problems.

In all fairness, each of us has the right to deal with things when we feel ready. And, as the lesson of our Chinese friend so aptly demonstrates, the infallibility of karma always prevails: what needs to come around will come around when the time is ripe. Thus, beyond the traditional deference that lay Buddhists are supposed to show monastics, I acknowledge them as men and women working out whatever they need to work out in the best way they know how.

Married People and Dishonorable Persons

According to the Tantric understanding of the subtle energetics of our body, emotions, and spirit, every time we get into bed with someone, and especially when we have intercourse while we're there, we come away from that bed with an energetic and psychic imprint. Later on, getting into bed with someone else, not only are we making love with that person, but the psychic imprints and energetic impressions of everyone else we have slept with go into that bed as well. Because of all these influences on our body and emotions, it becomes increasingly difficult to feel present, connected, and intimate with the person we are with.

Of course, it is commonly understood that prior sexual histories of rape and incest create tension and pain in relating sexually in the moment to someone we love or want to love. But any and all prior sexual encounters—be they in a drunken orgiastic frenzy, a one-night stand, or in the name of platonic or "friendly" sex—will add their own colors to the moment. Of course, these experiences can enrich us, giving us deeper awareness, appreciation, and skill; but they can also leave us confused about what we're experiencing and feeling here and now.

The truth of this is plain to anyone who's willing to look back and recall what it was like to make love for the first time. That experience, too, is still with us and informs us in the here and now. It is more deeply ingrained than we may have been willing to admit. Understanding this, we can more easily appreciate the Buddhist admonitions to avoid dishonorable people—those whose attitudes, actions, or medical histories could put us at risk physically, emotionally, or spiritually and forever taint our healthy and joyous sexual expression.

As the energetics of previous and present sexual encounters leave their marks, it is simply foolhardy to assume that secret liaisons and adultery would go undetected by our partner. We may be able to gloss things over or fake fidelity for a while. It's even possible to deceive the other for years. But we must realize that, at least on an energetic level, our Beloved will definitely feel that something has changed, perhaps without being able to put a finger on it. Not trusting his or her instinctual First Thought and wanting to believe in us, our partner may deny what is obvious. In any case, slowly and surely, good feeling and open expression within the couple will dissolve and, in turn, affect every relationship we have.

As will be elaborated further in the discussion on infidelity in chapter 11, rebuilding a relationship that has endured adultery is hard work. It requires restoring social and emotional confidence, as well as reestablishing trust at the physical level. For long after the adulterous events are over, beyond making amends, there is the task of allowing time to lessen the strength and attachment to those with whom we have committed the adultery. This includes clearing the memory of sexual encounters with them, which can still be felt energetically by the adulterer and the deceived partner. How long should this take? It is really an individual matter. Safely said, there are no shortcuts.

Not Tonight, Honey: Pregnant and Menstruating Women and Those with Weakening Conditions

How often has this line been used as a joke? Usually, the joke runs that the female partner is uninterested, there is something wrong that isn't being said, or there is some kind of sexual politics or manipulation happening.

With all of the stresses and strains that everyday life offers us, is it so unlikely that one of us would not be in the mood, whether we are male or female? If we honor the integrity of our partner and treat that person with the mutuality espoused by Buddhist masters and Gedun Chöpel in his *Tibetan Arts of Love,* to expect our partner to perform for our own satisfaction is both selfish and destructive to an enduring love.

For certain, there are emotional and intellectual reasons why one does not feel inspired to relate to one's partner sexually. At the same time, particularly in the course of a woman's sexual and reproductive life and health, there are factors that do come into play and, according to Tibetan Tantric medicine, must be considered: pregnancy and menstruation to be more specific. In these cases, not being in the mood may be a "good" thing, a reflection of a woman's sensitivity to her body's needs—especially from a medical and energetic point of view.

Because the Tibetan medical Tantras were primarily written by men (who were often celibate) in a society with a patriarchal bias, their perspective is definitely male. They therefore view men as the initiators and dominant characters in the dynamics of sexual interaction. However, despite this bias, the recommendations of these texts are designed to overcome the male tendency of not holding to monastic and Tantric laws or bending them in imposing themselves on women. The guidelines are also meant to ensure mutuality. Thus, where medical conditions that restrict sexual activity are discussed, emphasis is placed on feminine conditions that men should pay attention to with respect to their partner or lover. This material is far more extensive than that regarding male conditions.

According to the great contemporary Tibetan master Kalu

Rinpoche, pregnant women should be protected from sex because, once a child is conceived, the constant penetration of a male's penis shocks the fetus, and the semen released is experienced by the fetal child as the feeling of being burned.[3] It should be noted that other cultures, such as some Native American tribes, claim that semen is nurturing for the child. Is the Tibetan view as taught by monk doctors a result of their own sensitivity to sex in general? Or are those who teach the opposite just men justifying male desires and their right to have sex when and where they want it? Because of the cultural and situational nature of such restrictions or encouragements, this is a matter of personal discretion.

At the same time, most cultures agree that intercourse in late pregnancy is increasingly uncomfortable for the woman. There is even concern that pelvic and genital problems in the future may arise as a result. In his "Treatise on Passion" in *Tibetan Arts of Love,* Gedun Chöpel notes this restriction, but goes on to offer the desirous couples some useful hints for managing desire:

> If copulation can be given up, it is good. If it cannot, use methods of union from the side. If the stomach is pressed or the like when the womb has filled out, the limbs of the child will degenerate. In particular, as a thumb of the child stays around the nose, there is greater danger of developing a hare lip.[4]

Gedun Chöpel also makes the observation that during pregnancy, if a woman is particularly desirous of intercourse, this is a sign that the child in the womb is a female.[5]

As for menstruation, Tantric medical theory teaches that it is a process of cleansing best left uninterrupted. It is precipitated by the downward-moving winds of the woman's body. The upward-moving thrusts of a penis and the introduction of sperm swimming upstream are, therefore, counterproductive to proper cleansing.

Nevertheless, if both partners are inclined and view it as a time when they can relax around the issue of conception, menstruation may be a tempting time to have unprotected sex—provided they don't mind all the mess. My general advice has been to consider indulging at the beginning of the period before the flow really gets under way and at the end when the cleansing has basically come to an end.

However, according to other Tantric sources cited by Douglas and Slinger in their Western classic, *Sexual Secrets*, even that sort of precaution is unnecessary if the couple are mindful of their position for intercourse. The recommended position involves the man lying on his back and remaining relatively still while the woman straddles him and moves on top of him, showering down upon his *lingam* (his penis) her "red snow."[6]

With respect to women with weakening conditions or debilities, the issue of abstaining has to do in part with not taking advantage of someone in a weakened state. From a medical point of view, if a body that is weak and needs to rest is excited, the result is a further disturbance in the body's energy that can lead to more problems and a slower recovery.

At the same time, it should be noted that in both Taoist practice and Hindu Tantra, certain intercourse postures are considered therapeutic and restorative. The earlier reference to the Tibetan medical recommendations of intercourse for some psychiatric conditions suggests that even in this matter there is some level of agreement among various traditions. In all these traditions, intention, mutuality, and skill are important factors.

OTHER AVENUES OF SEXUAL INTENSITY

Foreplay and Oral Sex

Creating arousal through foreplay and engaging in other sexual acts that heighten desire are a part of what happens on the sexual playing field—and always have been. Thus, while Buddhist texts mainly discuss the essential sexual act of copulation and achieving orgasm in that way, other sexually arousing acts can also be understood in the light of a Buddhist sense of morality and the energetic principles of Tantric medicine.

Undoubtedly, foreplay and oral sex increase desire. In classical and contemporary Buddhist teachings, desire is considered a risky feeling to play with, as it can lead to attachment, which in turn leads to suffering. But, again, we are beings from a realm where desire is a part of what makes us who we are, and to cast it as the enemy and repress or deny its place in our lives is equally, if not more, risky.

Between two loving partners, deliberate arousal may be enjoyable and part of the mystery and joy they experience in passion. However, done to taunt, manipulate, or hold power over another without a sense of mutuality and caring, such acts create an attachment and energetic instability that can be harmful to another's equanimity, both physically and emotionally. Thus, intention, once again, becomes the culprit more than the acts themselves. From this standpoint, when Kalu Rinpoche was asked to comment on the practice of oral sex, he said:

> There is some basis for this prohibition in the teachings of the dharma. However, it seems to me that these are relatively minor points which we could let alone, and just let sentient beings in samsara be sentient beings in samsara. I am not going to get too particular about the whole thing.[7]

From the perspective of Ayurvedic medicine, the alignment of energies between a male and female in intercourse is balancing for both partners. Variations in posture may create different energetic effects, but all fall within a range that circulates the energy in a positive, healthy manner. With oral sex, the chakras and energy channels that are normally not connected—mouth to phallus, tongue to clitoris—are brought together, the result being heightened arousal and excitement. Whether this turns out to be "good" or "bad" depends on intention and on whether it brings joy to the relationship or just breeds greater intoxication and attachment in ways that are destabilizing.

In the context of foreplay in Tantric love, oral sex and the heightened heat of passion it arouses provide the practitioners with more aspects of consciousness and experience to explore and channel. To the Tantrika, as his or her partner is viewed as a female or male Buddha respectively, no part of the body is considered embarrassing or unclean; special words are used for genitalia that differ from the common conversational terms. Further, all bodily substances secreted are nectar. Tantric texts speak of drinking each other's seminal fluids, viewing them as elixirs of bliss and immortality.

Even if the uninitiated take this view to overcome embarrassment and just open up to this act as an expression of their loving nature, oral sex can become an expression that is positive and mutually nourishing in romantic love.

Erogenous Zones

In every dimension of life, the Buddhist sense of mindfulness can be applied. Thus, it is no surprise that in "The Treatise on Passion," Gedun Chöpel cites astrological data from Indian sources that spell out how movement of the subtle energy in a woman's body creates different erogenous zones on her entire body over the course of a lunar month.[8] I am including this material as it can go a long way to spicing up a couple's sex life in a way that is mutually pleasing for both partners. With foreplay, as in all matters, intention coupled with wisdom and skillful means yields favorable results. For men, knowing how to effectively arouse a woman rather than annoy her with the usual groping at preferred body parts does seem a worthy ambition.

According to this tradition, areas that are most arousing to a woman move in the following cyclic manner, based on the days of the lunar month (day 1 being the new moon and day 15, the full moon):

MONTHLY EROGENOUS ZONES CYCLE

Day	Area	Day	Area
1	calves	7	stomach
2	knees	8	chest
3	thighs	9	shoulders
4	pubic region	10	cheeks
5	waist	11	mouth
6	navel	12	nose

Day	Area	Day	Area
13	ears	22	chest
14	top of head	23	stomach
15	entire body	24	navel
16	top of head	25	waist
17	ears	26	pubic region
18	nose	27	thighs
19	mouth	28	knees
20	cheeks	29	calves
21	shoulders	30	upper part of feet

To stroke, kiss, caress, or suck these areas is to ensure that your partner experiences greater pleasure, hence increased desire. Unfortunately, Gedun Chöpel makes no reference to a similar list for arousing men.

Anal Sex

No doubt anal sex has always been practiced, but neither "The Treatise on Passion" nor any other Buddhist text I have come across makes mention of it. At the same time, as in the case of oral sex, such an act could be classified as "uncertain," as a different orientation is involved and a different orifice is being penetrated, the result yielding an energetic field unlike the one created during regular penile-vaginal intercourse.

Besides this energetic consideration, within the context of Buddhist spiritual practice, certain meditations and yogic acts require a tightening up of the anal muscles. Thus, the stretching of this sphincter in anal intercourse would be counterproductive. Furthermore, with the possibility of fecal contamination, the act carries its own set of health risks. One can get advice and find books and materials that address health concerns (many, for example, advocate the use of condoms in anal sex). In considering such an act, it seems wise to ask ourselves what our intention is and visualize what we'd like to see as the desired outcome. From a Buddhist point of view, the issue of mutuality remains the foremost consideration.

VIRILITY AND IMPOTENCE

The Tibetan medical Tantras include much discussion about the repression or excessive release of seminal fluid. In general, retention of seminal fluids helps to develop clarity, insight, power, and bliss. However, according to the Ayurvedic teachings from the Medicine Buddha, the amount and strength of the essence that is carried by seminal fluid varies from individual to individual based on constitutional strengths and weaknesses. It is further affected by our diet and lifestyle (including sexual activity), and the time of month, the season, and the year.

Semen is considered to be extremely rich in nutrients and, as mentioned previously, to possess vital energy drops, an essence known as tigle. In accordance with Tibetan medicine, Gedun Chöpel writes that seven drops of vital essence of food produce one drop of blood in a human body. A cup of blood goes into producing one drop of seminal fluid, distilled from the blood in the heat of passion.

When dual Tantra is practiced and the heat of passion creates concentrated seminal fluid that is drawn up rather than released, the tigle available in the fluid affects our entire psychophysiology and increases our experiences of insight and bliss. This is true for both men and women. Thus, retaining seminal fluid or at least regulating its release is recommended to tantrikas primarily because of the tigle that can be lost as an available resource for spiritual transformation. However, anyone of any gender engaging in sexual activity can benefit from such retention and regulation.

The textbook discussions of the debilities that result from holding this fluid through excessive physical force or releasing it too frequently are almost entirely devoted to men. When men repress ejaculation or forcefully retain seminal fluid, there can arise penile diseases, impotence, throbbing in the heart, testicular swelling (what guys call "blue balls"), pain in the limbs, difficulty with urination, disturbed eyesight, and other sensory debilities. Besides getting the semen out, Tibetan medical remedies include learning how to relax, indulging in only moderate amounts of alcohol, bathing in medicinal herbs, and including certain foods in the diet, such as chicken, beef, milk, millet, and sesame oil.[9]

The literature also describes how the frequency of ejaculation is supposed to vary according to season. In the winter, it is said that we can make love and ejaculate any time. During the springtime and summer, intercourse with seminal fluid release should happen no more than once every two weeks. In the fall, we can indulge every other day. Further, the amount of seminal fluid available to us at any given time also varies over the course of the lunar month. The result of expending this precious fluid in a random or excessive fashion, with no regard to season or time of the month, is a general weakening of vitality, diminishing of the senses, and quickening of the aging process.

The ebb and flow of our available sexual juices and vitality also affects our libido: "Sometimes you're hot. Sometimes you're not." Not knowing this and holding the expectation that we should be ready for passion day or night, whenever our partner gives a nod and a wink, is to set standards we cannot live up to. We end up sitting at the end of the bed, wondering why nothing happens or why it wasn't as great as last week.

We can do little to change our constitutions or alter the flow of months and seasons. However, we can do something about our lifestyle. A renowned Indian Ayurvedic physician, Dr. Sunil Joshi, tells men and women he consults with to be wary of three things: hurry, worry, and curry. Chaotic living, mental stress, and poor diet are the chief culprits in our daily experience of disease, and certainly causal factors in the most common sexual dysfunctions.

When we are young and virile, we can make love repeatedly all night long whenever we like. Our diet and lifestyle may be a bit sloppy, but the gift of youth creates in us the notion that we can misspend our energies with little repercussion. Over time, as increasingly serious jobs and other obligations crowd our days, the mind gradually develops the habit pattern of thinking one day, two days, three months, or a year ahead. Burdened by responsibility, we are hardly in the present.

We worry about what hasn't even happened. As this worry increases we find that, because we are so distracted, all we are doing here and now is suffering. The stress begins to affect our metabolism; our iron-stomach view of ourselves gives way as our digestion weakens. We start to lose or gain weight more easily. We try stimulants such as coffee and soft drinks to boost our energy and resort to alcohol or drugs to help us calm down and take the edge off our escalating edginess. Under these circumstances, when we come to make love, we are knotted up with concerns and so physically depleted from poor nutrition that enjoying the time together with our mate translates into a momentary orgiastic explosion followed by exhaustion born of tension and malnutrition.

But whatever our lifestyle, no matter what our constitutional strength or what amount of seminal fluid we were able to produce in our prime, aging changes everything. All things are impermanent. What has a beginning has an end. What we could do when we were young we don't seem to be able to do in the same fashion as we get older, even if we remain nineteen at heart. If we do manage to perform as we used to, chances are that our recovery rate for another go-round takes a little longer than it did.

Failing to realistically appraise our own strengths and weaknesses in the short or long term, we hang on to or desperately cling to obsolete images of ourselves and how we think we should behave or perform. All of this is reinforced by our well-marketed youth-obsessed culture, which encourages us to resist adapting gracefully to inevitable change. This is often the most bitter pill we have to swallow as we age. And in a culture that spends so much energy denying, demonizing, or deifying sexuality, it stands to reason that the loss of our virile image leaves the worst possible aftertaste.

And so, with a distorted vision of reality, endlessly disappointed in ourselves, we try to mold, pound, or snip at ourselves to create a freeze-dried image of whatever we perceive the right, attractive sexual image to be. For women, this might be expressed in getting breast enlargements or reductions, molded plastic forms for the right contoured buttocks, liposuction, the waxing off of excess pubic hair, or spraying crotches with toxic substances to deodorize and freshen that nasty human smell. For men, maybe it's getting a hair transplant or dye job or starting a belated exercise program; if all else fails, there's always a shunt that promises to keep a man erect, even in his grave.

None of these things is necessarily a sign of being shallow or vain. Some procedures may be medically warranted and can, in some conditional way, help with self-esteem and keeping a spark alive. Even in the medical Tantra texts, impotence and virility were considered matters that warranted attention. Certainly many recommendations were included to ensure a slowing of the aging process and a return to a greater level of sexual prowess.

The medical Tantras teach that it is possible to remain healthily virile and sexually active into our later years. Whereas, in the case of men, Western culture offers Viagra to force the body to activate the physical resources to get an erection—with unwanted side effects or collateral physical damage—the Medicine Buddha talks about diet, exercise, stress reduction, detoxification, and the taking of rejuvenating herbs and elixirs that rebuild the entire body, thus making it possible for an erection to come in a balanced, natural way. For women, similar lifestyle recommendations are given along with formulas to tone breast tissue, reduce wrinkling, and encourage healthy vaginal secretions.*

But these guidelines for bodily care also address a deeper purpose. According to Tibetan Ayurvedic medical tradition, the highest goal of rejuvenation and maintaining virility is to give us the resourcefulness, power, and energy to strengthen and develop our spiritual life. Well-bodied and full of life, we can still taste what it is like to be young and treasure what has passed—or at least what is no longer in plentiful supply. We can also provide engaging, compassionate friendship and guidance to those actively misspending their youth as we did. And,

---

* For further information see Melanie Sachs, *Ayurvedic Beauty Care* (Twin Lakes, Wis.: Lotus Press, 1994).

when it comes to the very end, having strengthened ourselves in this way, we will more easily maintain the focus necessary to die well.

> *The highest goal of rejuvenation and maintaining virility is to give us the resourcefulness, power, and energy to strengthen and develop our spiritual life.*

In an intimate relationship that matures over time, sexual activity is but one expression in the use of sexual energy. This energy informs our creativity; it generates sparks of interest, intensity, and playfulness in other areas of our lives. To equate its expression solely with blood-engorged genitals, throbbing stiffness, sweat, and orgasm is to deny an ebb and flow that can infuse a sense of warmth and joy in all we do with our Beloved.

Nonetheless, if it is possible to be locked in sexual embrace with my Beloved at the moment of death, what more blissful end to life together could there be? Perhaps this is an immature dream, one that reflects how little I know of the ecstasy of full enlightenment. But for now, this is one fantasy I don't mind holding on to.

Homosexual Love

Association with a mate—brought to one by the power of previous actions (karma)—with love like that for one's own dear life and with abandonment of intrigues and adultery is the best of ethics.

—GEDUN CHÖPEL, *TIBETAN ARTS OF LOVE* (P. 131)

In writings on Tantric love, it is obvious to the reader that the intercourse being discussed is heterosexual in nature, between a man and a woman. The term used for this act and shown in thangkas depicting the internal transformation of a tantrika is known in Tibetan as *yab yum*. Like the Chinese yin and yang or the *yoni* and *lingam* in Hindu practice, yab yum is the union of the male and female principles.

According to Buddhist teachings, the polarity of male and female energy is needed to properly perform dual Tantra; the penis and vagina serve as the most important ports of entry and exit. Thus, by definition, homosexual partners cannot perform dual Tantra as such. No doubt, the love that gay men and lesbian women have for each other can be as deep and significant as that of any heterosexual couple. The sex gay couples have can be physically and emotionally gratifying, even spiritually transforming with respect to shifts to a paradigm of greater openness and compassion. However, sexual stimulation and acts other than straight intercourse will never move energy and create the internal and external transformations of Tantric love. Of course, this does not exclude a gay person from being a tantrika, for as each of us possesses the energetics of the masculine and feminine anyone can learn individual Tantric meditative processes to achieve Tantric realization.

Ultimately, Buddhism holds that the important point for all beings is to find the means and path to reconnect with their loving nature. Thus, the *yab yab*s and *yum yum*s among us find within the teachings of the Buddha no judgment or condemnation. In meeting Buddhists from various cultures, we may experience some intolerance, even bigotry, but this has more to do with the cultures Buddhism finds itself in than with Buddhist teachings themselves. Even in the matter of Tantra, there is no true discrimination; the exception is based on the unalterable reality of human biology—nothing more.

The most powerful elucidation, perhaps, of the Buddhist perspective on homosexuality comes from the teachings of Korean Zen master Seung Sahn. In the early 1980s at an ecumenical conference where the issue of homosexuality and spirituality was being explored, Zen master Seung Sahn explained the following position, the logic of which is based on the concept and reality of reincarnation.

Imagine, if you will, that you have had countless incarnations since beginningless time. Over the millennia of your being, 75 percent of your incarnations were as a man and 25 percent as a woman. Thus, over all that time, in developing habitual patterns and preferences rooted in the Three Poisons, you have the predominant attractions and aversions of a male. But because of your tendencies and reactions to circumstances in your most recent past life or as a culmination of the same over many lifetimes, you currently find yourself in the body of a woman. Your consciousness, molded by uncountable impressions, however, leads you to have male inclinations and desires. You like to climb trees, are drawn to big motorbikes, and find yourself attracted to petite brunettes. The reverse of this scenario could be presented with respect to the inclinations and desires of a gay man.

Another dimension of this, as an extrapolation of Zen master Seung Sahn's premise, may be that in a previous life two people were heterosexual lovers, and that by the force of karma one in the couple was born into the body of the opposite sex—the female lover might become the boy next door—and as two males in the current incarnation, they can't take their eyes off each other. If it is true that we tend to get reborn in close proximity to those whose karmic bonds with us are strong and to reconnect with them in a new way, this scenario is quite plausible.

Zen master Seung Sahn's conclusion: What's the big deal? Why chastise, berate, or abuse those whose predicament may be less than usual but is, in the end, not that different from anyone else's? We all have karma and its precipitating habitual patterns to work out.

Culturally, however, we persist in making this matter a big deal. According to the teachings of Andrew Cohen, who as author of several books on enlightenment and director of the Impersonal Enlightenment Fellowship is recognized by both Buddhist and Hindu masters as a master in his own right, when we are born, one of the first things that is proclaimed about us is "It's a boy!" or "It's a girl!" We are identified first and foremost by our gender. This, in turn, sets off an entire cascade of cultural expectations of who we are to become over the course of our lives.

Cohen explains that one of the most critical existential dilemmas we face is that deep inside we know ourselves as beings with enlightenment potential, but this identity is at odds with our relative condition and place in a world reinforced by habit patterns, patterns that are both personal and collective. Enlightenment, he claims, is genderless. When we fully embrace our enlightenment potential and manifest as a Buddha incarnate, we have no thought other than to manifest in whatever form is necessary to help other beings. As Lama Ole Nydahl remarks, we then merely have a body rather than identify with our body. That the form be male or female is of no consequence.

> *"We feel our own body condense out of space. It is power and joy. Something essential has happened. Before, we were our body and thus vulnerable to old age, sickness, death, and loss. Now we have our body."*
>
> —LAMA OLE NYDAHL

However, we do identify with our body and gender, and in so doing we eclipse our potentials. Thus, in the process of cutting through habitual patterns and uprooting ego, one of the primary patterns that we need to clear—indeed, one of the primary building blocks of the ego—is our identification with our gender.

Does this mean that we become androgynous? No. When we incarnate with the energy inherent in skillful means, we manifest as male and best utilize our body recognizing those potentials it offers us. If we are primarily infused with wisdom, we manifest as female and work with another set of potentials.

What letting go of gender identification does mean is that we think and act authentically, no longer obsessed with performing the gender-identified roles of our culture—within obvious biological limits.

Cohen postulates that the dilemma of breaking out of gender constraints faces all of us regardless of gender or gender orientation. But in the case of homosexuals, compound this with a karmic reality whereby they inhabit a body that is not dominated exclusively by the usual gender patterns. Further, they live in a culture that neither understands nor feels compassion toward this divergence from the norm; worse, it is overtly intolerant of anything that differs from what the majority has defined and agreed upon as normal. This intolerance is further magnified in a culture whose definitions and rules in the realm of sexuality are immature or repressive or both.[1]

In such cultures, when the predominant distinguishing factor between a straight person and a gay person comes down to sexual attraction and preference, it often happens that gay individuals are judged strictly in terms of this distinction, rather than being seen as whole, multidimensional beings. A gay person may be smart, friendly, considerate, and an exemplary taxpayer; nonetheless, this single dimension of sexual preference not only overrides but negates these other attributes altogether. It is the standard by which homosexuals are judged and becomes the standard by which they judge themselves.

Thus, society's intolerance coupled with gay people's internalized sense that nothing else in their character matters to others wreaks havoc on two levels: it creates the illusion that the sex and sexual preferences of gay people are somehow threatening or dangerous to society, and it elevates these factors to a degree of obsession within the gay community. Such a situation perpetuates ignorance, gets reinforced by fear, and results in alienation. It creates an "in the closet" or "in your face" reality.

Even those who have felt gay their entire lives have seldom been able to display these tendencies with no inhibitions. By far the greatest inhibiting factor that keeps them from openly revealing their tendencies is that they observe how different their attractions and aversions with respect to desire and affection are from those of the heterosexual people around them. This in itself can be the cause of a good deal of confusion that leads them to be more introspective, sensitive, and even guarded as they learn what is acceptable and unacceptable in word and action. Depending on the spaciousness and sensitivity of family, peers, and the society around them, they gradually work through their own labyrinth—which is inherently more challenging at a basic biological and emotional level than that of their heterosexual friends. If the environs they find themselves in are not so tolerant and if they do not have the space, opportunity, or inner resources to open up to their loving nature as it expresses itself in the body and mind they currently reside in, self-doubt and self-loathing may grow to a pathological degree. Every nuance in gesture and communication becomes charged with messages of acceptance or rejection.

All this said, Western culture at this time appears to be more tolerant of its gay members than it has at any time in the recent past. Fundamentalist and other puritanical elements of society claim that this is due to the depravity of our modern world, the decline in morality. However, I would like to postulate that this phenomenon has less to do with morality and more to do with a breakdown in cultural boundaries and definitions. Gay people have always been with us. As definitions and boundaries of norms become less operational in the cultural mix of most modern, nonhomogenous societies, personal preference becomes possible as a legitimate criterion for building a lifestyle based on our own sense of who we are.

Of course, there is still a level of discomfort with gays that is evident in a predominantly heterosexual world. Thus, as for all minorities that are held suspect but must be tolerated by reason and law, enclaves are established where gays can be as expressive in public as their heterosexual counterparts. That legislators, lobbyists, and intelligent arts and a sensitive media help to break through the barriers fueled by suspicion and fear is a testimony to the triumph of our intrinsic loving nature over the limitations we impose on ourselves when ruled by the Three Poisons. The religious and moral hype of puritanical individuals and groups against the gays and their so-called infecting of society is pure homophobia. It's based thoroughly on a lack of understanding and the commitment to hold to that lack.

If we are to hold to what Zen master Seung Sahn says, then being gay is a karmic reality that we must honor and work with just as we do any other karmic pattern that arises. We all benefit from tolerating, perhaps even delighting in, another variation in the display of human affection. But, if what Andrew Cohen says is right, that our gender and gender orientation are primary to the ego sense of who we are, it stands to reason that a homosexual embrace could feel threatening to heterosexuals. The threat here, however, is not to our own sexuality and sexual preferences, but rather to our own fixations and habitual patterns. It is a call to awaken.

Being in the Moment
and Killing the Moment:
Reflections on Matters That
Can Harm Intimacy

*The strongest form of attachment seems to be
sexual attachment. Here we find attachment
toward all five senses involved. Therefore, it is
all the more powerful and has the potential
for problems and destruction.*
—His Holiness the Dalai Lama, *The Dalai Lama's*
Book of Daily Meditations (p. 217)

When I first met my wife, Melanie, we played 100 questions. Actually, it wasn't play. It was the courtship ritual we engaged in. And in fact, it was Melanie who asked most of the questions.

Sitting on a hillside overlooking the English countryside, Melanie began to ask me about how I saw the world and what I wanted from a relationship. Both of us had just emerged from relationships that left us feeling very cautious about meeting anyone new, let alone embarking on an intimate relationship.

But here we were. The feelings were there. Attraction was happening. And we just didn't want to land in the same old soup once more. Hence, 100 questions.

I guess I answered them right. More important, it set a precedent for our relationship. Since that time we cherish the moments we have to reflect on what matters most to us, and what could get in the way of our love if left unattended.

In the heat of passion and even in the enduring warmth of affection over time, there are certain matters to which we must pay extra attention and which require reflection, deepened understanding, and resolution. In particular, I refer to three matters that directly involve our sense of feeling secure in our expression of sexuality and our comfort around and responsibility for our reproductive capabilities: incestuous feelings, abortion, and contraception.

> *In the heat of passion and even in the enduring warmth of affection over time, there are certain matters to which we must pay extra attention and which require reflection, deepened understanding, and resolution.*

Incestuous feelings, contraception, and abortion will, in one form or another, arise as issues in any intimate relationship. Needless to say, issues around incest and child abuse are probably some of the most poignant topics with which psychiatrists, psychologists, and psychotherapists work with their clients. And both religious and legal institutions are continuously wrangling around the issues of abortion and forms of accepted contraception. As a family man in community and as a professional therapist, I have seen that any one of these three matters can arise in, challenge, and often devastate a relationship.

As we get close to another, how our sexuality has been acknowledged and allowed to develop as a part of our personal expression by our parents and others close to us affects how timid or bold we are in presenting ourselves to our Beloved. Once we get close enough that sparks fly and intimate moments arise, we discover how comfortable we feel about going forward with reckless abandon and, if not, how we address and manage any strategies to impede the possibility of conceiving without spoiling the moment. Where does our partner stand? What if we do conceive? Does our Beloved embrace our thoughts about whether to go forward with or to terminate a pregnancy?

> *How our sexuality has been acknowledged and allowed to develop affects how timid or bold we are in presenting ourselves to our Beloved.*

When we think of the Buddhist meditative concept of "being in the moment," there is often the assumption that somehow critical thinking is absent. After all, don't we want to be spontaneous? Isn't spontaneity about stepping forward, taking a risk to be in the moment?

It is. But, spontaneity is based on a contemplative and meditative awareness. It arises from a freshness that is not tainted by habitual thought. Thus it arises with awareness and intelligence. Indeed, it is the exact opposite of impulsiveness.

Of course, some of you may belong to a religious group that has

strong values with which both you and your Beloved are in 100 percent agreement. But, more than likely, that is not your situation. Thus,
if one wants to "be in the moment," one needs to be willing to self-
reflect and communicate about these matters. To be in the moment as
far as sexual intimacy is concerned means that if we want to be able
to be in the moment later on down the road or in bed with our Beloved, we need to be aware of how we feel about each of these matters.
Otherwise, without much attention, these matters will spontaneously
raise their heads, challenge us, and perhaps even kill the moment.

It is my intention in this chapter to offer a Buddhist perspective that
one can contemplate and discuss with one's partner. With compassion
and a sense of mutuality, all of these matters can be addressed in a
way that not only does not inhibit true spontaneity but can, in fact,
help us to be more daring in embracing our Beloved and the intimacy
that it is possible to share.

INCESTUOUS FEELINGS

Much contemporary self-help literature in the West that focuses on
personal mental health devotes some time to the subject of incest.
Indeed, incest can clearly be identified as cause for much psychologi-
cal wounding that may require years for the one who was violated to
work through. Because of this, there is no guarantee that he or she
will resolve this issue before embarking upon intimate relationships
with others.

   Although it is unclear how common a problem incest is in our
culture, the attention it receives does indicate that we have become
sensitized to its significance and that it must be addressed as a factor
impacting intimacy and our lives in general. As such, the topic of
incestuous feelings—often the precipitating factor in various forms of
abuse, including emotional, physical, and sexual—seems warranted.
The Buddhist understanding of these feelings, which may at first glance
seem both provocative and controversial, has the potential, in my
opinion, to be of great benefit to those who must deal with this mat-

ter personally, whether as perpetrator or victim, or as witness for partners, friends, or clients.

> *The Buddhist understanding of
> incestuous feelings has the poten-
> tial to be of great benefit to those
> who must deal with this matter
> personally, whether as perpetra-
> tor or victim, or as witness for
> partners, friends, or clients.*

Conception happens when three factors come together: an ovum, a
sperm cell, and the consciousness of a being who wants to be born
that enters into the mix.

According to Buddhist spiritual and medical tradition, after we
die it is our karma that determines when, where, and in what manner
we will once again manifest. With the exception of beings who are
already enlightened or have the good fortune to awaken to their
Buddhanature and achieve liberation in the bardo—or in-between state
after death and before rebirth—it is said that most of us are reborn
within forty-nine days of our death. For this reason, *The Tibetan Book
of the Dead* is read to the deceased throughout that time. The purpose of this is to provide instructions for liberation or at least for
achieving a better rebirth.

As we approach the time of rebirth, what grabs our attention is
the energy pattern or vibrational frequency that is created by the
lovemaking of our future parents. If the consciousness we possess has
predominantly male impressions and habitual patterns, then we are
attracted to the woman making love—not as a mother, but as a potential lover. A consciousness with female impressions and habitual
tendencies responds to the man. We get attracted to the scene of

lovemaking as if we, ourselves, were going to make love. We soon find out different, ending up swimming around in amniotic fluid.

In this factual manner, Buddhist teaching explains incestuous feelings between parents and children. Whereas Dr. Freud wanted to attribute the Oedipal and Electra complexes to our parents at this time—thus laying the burden of feelings and acts of incest in the laps of our parents in this lifetime exclusively—the Buddha shows us that these feelings are the result of inevitable habitual patterns that come about and are reinforced lifetime after lifetime. Because we have been mother, father, sister, brother, and lover to one another since beginningless time, the attraction we have for one another is deeply rooted, and sufficient cause for coming back again and again.

To illustrate how Buddhism looks at the phenomenon of incestuous feelings, I would like to share a personal story . . .

I became friends with Melanie's grandmother toward the end of her grandmother's life. Because Nana and Melanie were so close, I daresay that my inclusion into the family and my becoming a very welcome visitor for Nana was almost a given. After all, if Melanie liked me, I must be all right. And as time went on, I would say that Nana and I shared a special, mutual affection.

Nana was legally blind and nearly totally deaf. For the most part she stayed in one room in her daughter's home. She could barely walk and her breathing was labored, creating the necessity for her to receive a great deal of medication. Because of my background in alternative medicine, I sometimes helped her with her pain and her breathing. And my Buddhist perspective was also helpful, particularly one time when Nana had grown fearful of various people who she said came and went from her room. Her daughter swore that there were no visitors. And yet, Nana reported that she had a constant bevy of gents and ladies who came by to visit. When I told her that according to Buddhist thinking most of the 84,000 kinds of beings in the universe were invisible, she clutched my hand in glee and shouted, "Oh, what a relief." And from that time on, she could relax and converse with her visitors or not, depending on her fancy. Over a span of just a couple of years, Nana's condition worsened. Melanie and I elected to move back to England to help Melanie's mother and be close to Nana. We were not long returned to the U.K. before Nana was admitted to the hospital. In that time, Melanie, our daughter, and I visited her regularly. And although we were not present on the morning that she died, we sensed her passing.

Within the year, Melanie and I conceived a child. Our second daughter was born on January 15, the birthday of Nana. To honor her spirit, we decided to give her Nana's first name, Harriet.

According to the Buddhist tradition as it is practiced in the East, we tend to reincarnate near people or circumstances we have a close karmic bond to. This means that we may even reincarnate in our own families, where, for most of us, our karmic links are the strongest. For some of us, this may be of comfort, for others, maybe not.

In any event, our daughter Harriet began to show just how much she was like her namesake at a very early age. She named one of her stuffed pets Tibbles, a name that Nana had used. Her food likes and dislikes were certainly not in keeping with what we ate. She loved all the foods that Nana liked, especially mashed potatoes. As she grew, she loved to bake—especially cookies. Nana spent her youth and middle age working in a bakery. Whenever Melanie has gone out of town, Harriet wants to take over the house, to take on the role of mother (much to the annoyance of her brother). And yes, Harriet and I are very close.

For both Melanie and me, how we have seen our daughter grow is mixed with a sense of old familiarity and new possibility. After all, even though a person may have been a certain way in a past life, every new day gives the opportunity to change patterns and go in new directions. As the great female Buddhist master Khandro Rinpoche has said, "If you want to know whom you were in a past life, just look at your life today." Where you are and whom you are with is no mystery. The only mystery is what you will do with those potentials here and now. Only this will determine what, where, and whom you will be with in the future.

Whether the man or woman a potential baby girl or boy is attracted to when becoming conceived is their former child, lover, or parent, Buddhist teaching sees the reality of a sexual attraction being the hook that, once more, brings the boy child to his mother and the girl child to her father. And so a little girl is fascinated by and attracted to the power of her daddy and longs to be the apple of his eye. Later on, she'll "strut her stuff," testing her developing sexual identity with her father. A little boy wants to show his mommy how manly and strong he is. Later on, he'll become the zealous protector of his mother's virtue.

However the expression may manifest in any given culture, the roots of such feelings are karmic; they are a part of becoming. Parents can learn to nurture and support their children in profound ways by understanding the origins of incestuous feelings and accepting sexual attraction as a dimension inherent in the daughter-father or son-mother relationship. This enables their children, in turn, to experience the love and safety within which they can mature and move into independence. They learn to trust their own loving nature and to display affection toward others in appropriate ways.

Without the recognition of the biological and habitual nature of incestuous feelings, their repression and denial become the breeding ground for any number of neurotic preoccupations—up to and including forms of abuse. Some cultures in the world actually encourage fathers to have intercourse with their daughters in order to instruct them in the ways of men and how men should behave toward them. Whether this is a cultural rationalization or not, it certainly doesn't involve denial. At the same time, I do not believe incestuous feelings need to be acted on in order for us to accept and integrate them in consciousness and action. Properly worked through and seen for what they are, such feelings give way to the specialness of the bond between son and mother or daughter and father; this remains and becomes the backdrop from which children can develop a relaxed and healthy perspective on their own sexuality and have a better sense of the bond they are seeking with a mate.

The Buddha taught that we should have unconditional love for our parents for all that they have done for us to keep us alive and in giving us this opportunity to be in this life. However, in keeping with the great Buddhist teacher Gampopa's words about special friends—that we can identify with our absolute, unconditional loving nature while recognizing our personal preferences and our tendencies toward greater affinity with certain people—we can unconditionally love someone without necessarily being able to relate to or live with them. There is no contradiction in this. The Buddhist distinction between unconditional and relative is useful when considering the dilemma some may face when looking at the cultural notions of loving and respecting one's parents in the face of having survived horrendous acts of abuse.

In this light, I encourage incest survivors to look more closely at their experience and the thoughts and feelings around their experience. You may have been in a situation where incestuous feelings were not handled skillfully and you were abused as a result. The Calm Abiding meditation and the meditation where you visualize the one you have difficulty with sitting beside you can be powerful tools. At the same time, beyond meditation and spiritual instruction, Buddhist teachers have often needed to be good counselors. Thus, one should not shy away from also seeking out competent counselors and psychotherapists who are trained to address these matters with you. You may never be able to fully forgive your parent for what he or she has done. But, if you understand that such feelings are a natural part of how we come to be in this world and approach your experience of this with meditation and contemplation, acceptance and compassion may soften your burden.

ABORTION

The act of taking a life in any circumstance is one we need to approach with wisdom and skillful means. In effect, it is a wrathful act, when, for whatever reason, we see the necessity to bring to an end a life for the benefit of some greater purpose—the preservation of life in a much greater context. This can include the acts of killing to eat, killing to protect oneself and/or others, or killing for some other greater good. As such, in any of these circumstances, we need to be clear about our intentions, and we need to acknowledge with reverence the life we are about to take.

If we don't have clear intentions, and if we try to deny to ourselves or others the preciousness of the life that we have taken, then we run the risk of losing touch not only with our own humanity but with life itself.

Abortion is a topic that is currently dividing this country. It has become a spiritual issue with political and economic repercussions. In fact, the sanction of abortion by the United States government was cited by some evangelistic and fundamentalist religious leaders as the reason the Twin Towers in New York were attacked on September 11. Abortion is a topic that makes its way into the selection and nomination of every elected official in the United States, even at the level of local school boards.

What I venture to present here is a Buddhist Middle Way approach to looking at this most heated topic. For I do believe that there is a place and path between the extremes of militant right-to-lifers and ardent pro-choicers that is both sane and well considered.

The loss of a child—either by abortion, miscarriage, stillbirth, or sudden infant death—is a significant factor in couples losing connection and confidence in their relationships. Thus, no comprehensive book on relationships can skirt the thorniness of what such circumstances or choices bring to the relationship table. My hope is that my treatment of what follows offers a compassionate, well-reasoned perspective from which to make difficult choices.

> *The loss of a child—either by abortion, miscarriage, stillbirth, or sudden infant death—is a significant factor in couples losing connection and confidence in their relationships.*

At that moment of conception when the egg, sperm, and consciousness come together, the spark of sentient life is ignited and begins. What will happen in the nine months of gestation that follow is the biological unfoldment of that internal spark. From the Buddhist point of view, that spark is no less human than the baby that develops from it.

Abortion, consequently, is considered killing. This is an undeniable fact. But rather than approach this act in the black-and-white terms often used in the current religious and political debates about this issue, Buddhism looks at this matter pragmatically.

One of the most important of general precepts that a moral Buddhist person embraces is not to kill. Killing in any form leads to negative consequences. However, what those consequences will be is determined by the situation, consciousness, and intent of the one who does the killing. The killing with the fewest negative consequences happens by accident, with no premeditation, and with regret in the aftermath. The killing with the most severe negative consequences involves planning and carrying out a murder and taking pleasure in the act. Between these two extremes there exists a wide range of circumstances, intents, and emotional responses.

Abortion can fit anywhere on the continuum. There are many motivators for abortion, but for the most part it's chosen because of health concerns or social and economic realities. We will now look at some of the scenarios in which it occurs, beginning with health reasons.

There are times when a pregnancy puts the mother's life at risk. If a child is the cause of the mother's death, that child will have to live with the karma created as a result. Who knows how he or she will be able to face the burden of this truth—whether told about it or not. In light of this reality, a mother who knows that her life is at risk might decide to abort with the conscious willingness to take the burden of the death of her child upon herself; in this case, in truth, she is sparing her child such a burden.

Of course, the motivating factor may be that the mother cherishes her own life and is afraid of dying or not ready to die. Who could honestly chastise her for not giving her own life for her unborn child? For certain, we must not rule out the possibility that a mother might be willing to sacrifice herself for the birth of her child. Because of our instinctive self-cherishing, anyone choosing this option would seem extraordinary. In karmic terms, however, because it would be virtuous to offer one's life to save another, this may be considered the most spiritually evolved action to take in a very difficult situation. Even if a society were to condone such an attitude and action (and ours largely does not), unless the mother were in total agreement with this view, the amount of coercion required to persuade her to follow this course would have its own consequences.

In other health-related cases, modern technology allows early detection of many birth defects and pregnancy complications that virtually guarantee a child will never come to full term. The longer intervention is avoided, the greater the risk to the mother—as in an ectopic pregnancy. With respect to defects, what do we do when we know the child will be severely deformed or retarded? Would it be considered an act of kindness to allow such a being to live out his or her life in this state?

This is a complicated matter; it affects parents, families, and entire societies. And anything so loaded always calls forth ecclesiastical and intellectual commentary. Abortion issues constitute one of the major battlefields between religion and science in the West. Those cloistered as upholders of faith do battle with those in secular ivory towers. Their arid debates often overlook the nitty-gritty reality altogether as the line is drawn between those who view as hallowed every form and shape born under God's sun and those who believe it is their job to genetically weed out defective human beings whose lives seem to serve no purpose or normal social function. Between divine detachment and scientific hubris live those of us who have to face and live in the reality of what it means on a day-to-day basis to support such offspring.

I have seen parents and siblings lovingly care for children with tremendous handicaps. There are also any number of care facilities throughout the world that cater to the needs of children with very particular needs. For the parents, siblings, and other caregivers who tend to these children, love, compassion, and understanding can grow in ways that other situations may not have made possible. In this way, these children come as gifts that serve our spirits and the blossoming of our loving nature.

However, in some cases, the emotional toll on parents can be overwhelming. The same is true for the financial responsibility of tending to such children in the home or in an institution that they will never leave. Savings become drained and resources for other members of the family shrink, often destroying the dreams of both the parents and their other children and creating an insurmountable state of destitution.

In cases of institutionalization, if benevolent medical and social service agencies determine that the family cannot or should not bear the financial burden involved, the cost for the care and technological support required to maintain or keep such children alive—often a small fortune—gets passed along to all health care consumers in the form of higher medical costs and insurance rates. This (combined with other high-dollar medical interventions) has an adverse effect on large sectors of the population and can make it too costly for many to receive adequate services. This fosters a resentment that is usually focused—and rightly so—on the medical industry and its number crunchers.

Of course, one may argue that the burden to care for those in such dire states belongs to society. What is important here is to keep the dialogue open on such matters as health care reforms and to place more importance on prevention and wellness as a means to create healthier, stronger pregnancies. If the moral dilemmas around abortion bring us to a point in our society where we no longer provide any legal sanction for it, how can we best help parents and families survive healthily in the context of losing mothers or caring for children experiencing a wide range of disabilities?

With respect to abortions of potentially healthy children that are sought because of emotional or economic stress, or if abortion is used as a convenience (as when a woman decides she is not ready for or just doesn't want a child right now), it behooves society to encourage adoption as the preferred alternative when a woman is capable of carrying a child to term and willing to do so. Then again, a woman may see this as an unacceptable route based on habitual patterns, including how she defines herself in her own world, and thus conclude that abortion is her only option. In terms of karmic ramifications based on what motivates our decisions, the worst fallout probably results when abortion is used as a method of contraception.

In all of the scenarios in which a woman would choose to have an abortion, regardless of circumstance or intent, I have never met a woman who did not have some degree of remorse and grief for her decision to abort a child. It is not uncommon for these feelings to cause strain in her relationship with the would-be father, or even to bring it to a painful end. And the risk of such painful circumstances arising again should she get too close to another man can become a dominant factor in her inability to engage with a partner in a truly intimate way.

Thus, in no case have I seen abortion be an easy decision to make or to live with for any woman. As we are beings who are by nature altruistic, our loving nature leads us to grieve over painfully difficult choices—which are based on our habitual patterns and what we know of the world at the point the decisions are made. The issue then becomes how best to integrate the experience into our lives in such a way that it does not shut us down, but rather opens us up to greater resourcefulness and wisdom in the future.

We must learn how to integrate the experience of difficult choices into our lives in such a way that it does not shut us down, but rather opens us up to greater resourcefulness and wisdom in the future.

To help them move forward in this way, I have encouraged women and, whenever possible, couples to create a ritual of completion with the child they chose to abort. For this being came to them by the sheer force of the karma between the three of them—mother, father, and him or her who sought rebirth with them. There is a relationship that needs to be acknowledged and brought to some form of peaceful resolution. Without a clear ending, the ghosts and memories of such an event will continue to linger.

As a final note on abortion, I look at the current U.S. administration's policy on not funding any foreign planned parenting programs that include abortion as one of their options. To my mind, this decision is based on narrow religious views and a sentiment around killing that is shortsighted. It does not factor into the equation any long-term ramifications.

Teaching the concept of contraception in foreign countries can be a tricky endeavor. In particular, instruction on the more successful forms of contraception, such as the Pill, presupposes an understanding of timing and an appreciation for daily adherence to a prescription. Then there are a host of cultural taboos that may make sexual planning something that is embarrassing or demeaning and kills spontaneity; people in other cultures may have any number of responses that we wouldn't guess at. Still, people are well aware of the consequences of having a child or another child in their lives. Abortion, in these situations, becomes a last, but often seemingly necessary, solution. In the matter of killing in this context, people often do not wish to kill, see no options, perform the deed, and live with varying degrees of regret.

Consider the alternative, whereby more unwanted children are born into regions of limited resources. Families, clans, or nations may literally go to war to get more resources for their swelling population. Consider the premeditation of battle planning, going into battle, and finally attaining some relief in vanquishing their enemy and living with the satisfaction that at least they did the best they could for their own. In such a scenario, abortion has been avoided, replaced by the sanctioned and morally justified killing of multitudes. Personally speaking, I would prefer to help women and their mates on a one-to-one basis to integrate a difficult choice into their lives than to deal with a nation of people experiencing the trauma of slaughter, whether as victims or victors. This is the matter that is not properly addressed when the abortion issue is looked at from a global perspective.

CONTRACEPTION

It's 1:30 a.m. and you have both just gotten home from a beautiful evening out. The dinner was superb, the wine just right, and the concert such a turn-on. You can hardly wait to get upstairs to the bedroom. This is a night for reckless abandon, a night when you want to turn each other on so much that it steams up the windows!

Babysitter paid and out of the way, you playfully run into the bedroom, looking forward to each moment of titillation to follow. You pull at each other's clothes, giggling and grunting with pleasure as you hear each pop of a button, each zip of a zipper, feeling the contours of each of your swollen parts. Each caress becomes more deliberate, more intense as you stumble enraptured toward the bed. And then each of you has a moment. The pause hits you both with the hard knock of reality.

"What about, you know, birth control?" he asks.

"Yeh," she sighs, remembering only last week that she decided to come off the Pill. After all, it made her feel swollen and moody. Wouldn't foam and condom be less of a problem? But what a hassle.

The thought of "hassle," an intrusion into the flow of certain bliss, brings things to a halt, but not quite.

"Let's just be a bit more careful," he says. After all, if he doesn't ejaculate inside her . . .

"I don't think I could handle that right now," she says breathless, but trying to control herself.

The intensity of the moment begins to fizzle into heated annoyance and a gruffness takes the place of playfulness. Neither of them wants to hurt the other, but it is clear that there is disappointment on both sides of the bed.

He rolls over with deep sighs, slowly trying to clear his head. She turns over and softly cries. Neither of them sleep well that night.

Or, what if . . .

Our lovers decide to go for it.

In the morning, with the heat of the moment gone, she reflects, "Well, I hope that was okay. I'm really not ready for another child."

The weeks go by and the anxiety about whether she'll start her period builds, both for her *and* for him. They're managing well with one child, but each of them is aware of the time, money, and attention another child would demand. Anxiety blends with moodiness and being snappy with each other.

Two days later than usual, her period begins. But those last two days of waiting felt like an eternity. It was hard to keep one's mind on work, on driving—just the thought, "What if . . . what if . . . what if . . ."

Using contraception to influence when one will have a child, or not, plays a large role in the dynamic of most modern Western couples. Even if there are cultural or religious taboos around the inhibition of the reproductive process in sexual activity, I have never met anyone who has a neutral opinion on the matter of conceiving or not. That being the case, contraception presents us with ethical, medical, and emotional issues that we need to explore with our partner.

The Mind and the Moment

Before addressing the issue of contraception itself, I would like to first discuss the issue of the intrusion of contraception as depicted in the story above and the mind-set that we start with when looking at this complex issue. For this is more the domain of Buddhist practice, as opposed to Buddhist philosophy and ethics.

In the beginning of this chapter we spoke of "being in the moment" and "killing the moment."

When in the throes of passion, or any intense situation for that matter, habitual mind—the domain of the Three Poisons of ignorance, attachment, and aggression—creates a pathway, a beginning and an end point to what one wants and the path one treads to get there. The more emotional heat there is, the more aggressively one tends to move along the path to the desired outcome. Anything that steps onto that path in an unexpected way is an unwelcome guest and thus gets dealt with quickly and pushed out of the way so that the course is laid clear for the awaited climax.

Such emotionally passionate moments reflect a more animal-like, instinctive response, a reflexive action that is not governed by logic. And yet, unlike our animal friends, we humans have a greater sense of consequence and possibility. We have such a wide array of things we are responsible for in our lives. All of us like to be carried away at times, to feel the intensity of life pulsing through us. At the same time, we also have the desire to be able to control that flow, whether it be for some long-term goal to benefit ourselves later on down the road or to help others.

Does this mean we have to abandon the heat, the passion, and the fun to be sensible, law-abiding, and predictably boring?

Not at all.

What we need to do is to look at whatever intrusion comes upon our path, such as dealing with contraception, as *part of the path.*

> *What we need to do is to look at whatever intrusion comes upon our path, such as dealing with contracep- tion, as* part of the path.

When we set in our minds what we want and what we don't want in a sexual encounter, then our intention and mindfulness can make anything a part of the path. Stopping to put on or put in contraception can be one of the playful dimensions of lovemaking. If condoms dull stimulation in one way, is it possible to turn one's attention to another dimension, another sensation?

What kills the moment most is meeting the moment with expectations and attachments to predictable outcomes. Free the mind of the expected, loosen the grip of attachment to what one is expecting to achieve or experience, and the experience becomes so much richer, so much more alive. The mind, with the practice of mindfulness as laid out in Buddhist practice, sees freshness in anything that arises. Being in the moment has more to do with embracing what the moment offers than trying to make the moment conform to how we want it to look. Even if we are looking down the road at a great night of sex, for us to meet that time with the wide eyes of openness creates more mystery, magic, and romance than trying to get it right, to make it all happen just the way we want.

> *Being in the moment has more to do with embracing what the moment offers than trying to make the moment conform to how we want it to look.*

With this foremost in our minds, let us look more closely into the various dimensions of contraception and how it influences us individually, as couples, and within the context of our culture as a whole. For each of these dimensions has an effect on our intimacy and our relationship to the world around us.

To Conceive or Not to Conceive

To look at contraception properly, we need to look at some basic facts about conception itself.

Having unprotected sexual intercourse with a full emission of semen does not guarantee conception. The reasons for this are not always medical. According to Buddhist teaching, there can be no baby if no one waiting to incarnate is drawn to the couple at the time of lovemaking. Thus, failure to conceive can be the karma of a particular biological event between a man and a woman, or the fact that there is no being with the appropriate karmic link attracted to the event, or both. Nature has its own methods of *contra*-ception—conditions that run counter to conception.

Why do some people oppose contraception on principle? Could it be that only couples who use nature's methods of contraception are righteous because they demonstrate a willingness to risk conception? Are only those who are willing to risk conceiving having righteous sex? If they do not conceive even if they do not believe in or use contraception, is their lovemaking a sin? Could there be people out there who shake their heads at happy people fornicating and applaud a couple's joy only if they do conceive? In some religious circles the sad answer is probably yes. Should people who don't or can't conceive consider themselves to be sinners if they continue to have sex? Again, sadly, some probably do.

Choosing to implement some strategy to block conception adds the element of choice into the mix. This is where the controversy supposedly lies. It's not about contraception itself—for nature has its own methods for blocking the creation of life. Rather, it is the human intervention that is particularly vexing to some and considered morally reprehensible.

Yet if we look at our world more closely, we see that at virtually every level of our biological involvement on this planet we make population decisions. We spay and castrate our pets. We select which cows and bulls, mares and stallions, hens and roosters will be allowed to breed and which ones won't—thus ending up more quickly on our tables or in our closets. We thin out wild herds of animals, claiming that if we don't there will be a population problem detrimental to the animals themselves. We create terminator seeds for crops. In other words, we are constantly willfully intervening in the reproduction of almost every species on this planet.

Some of these actions come from an agreed-upon common sense that many cultures share. Some come from the disturbing religious belief that we humans have been ordained and sanctioned to have dominion over all other forms of life. Just below God are the humans, made in God's image. Proponents of this viewpoint cite Scripture to substantiate these assertions. Magnificent portrayals of this logic can be found in Daniel Quinn's book *Ishmael* and the films *The Matrix* and *Instinct*.

If there is moral justification for human intervention into the lives of all creation, then to deny the value of contraception for humans is to consider ourselves exempt from what applies to all other life forms. This seems a highly suspect premise upon which to base our ethics.

His Holiness the Dalai Lama and other socially and politically minded Buddhist teachers state that one of the most obvious problems we as humans face is overpopulation. Still, many people hold lofty and sentimental notions about the biblical injunction still so often used at weddings to "be fruitful and multiply"—people ranging from wealthy churchgoers in spacious mansions, condos, and walled communities to those uninformed masses who are often the watchdogs for dogma. However, if any of those people were to spend some time in a ghetto, whether it be in their nearest major city or some third world country where sixteen live in a single room and others fight for cardboard boxes to sleep in on the streets, their view might change. But even beyond what is seen in poverty-stricken lands, the sheer number of people overall is taxing the natural resources on this planet. The result is an inevitable shortage of food, clothing, and shelter. Suffering increases and with it the tendencies for greater unrest and violence.

Unless there is some form of organized intervention into a population spiraling out of control, we will see a growing number of those who live below the poverty line. Of course, wars and unrest may be the only way to deal with and counter the effects of the excessive greed of multinational corporations and fascist politicians. They can certainly be effective ways to reduce population.

Overpopulation can also bring about various forms of natural disasters, plagues, famines, and other forms of pestilence that function, in turn, to destroy huge segments of human population. AIDS is doing just that to the Indian and African populations at the time of this writing. In my more cynical moments, I tend to think that such matters are not being looked at too closely by politicians, economists, or the media. Beyond racism as an obvious possible factor, as we are fast growing short on available land and resources, wouldn't the annihilation of large populations make lands available for development, mining, and so on?

When we weigh the morality of allowing the current state of affairs to continue—a guarantee that ever larger populations will experience the misery of poverty—versus actively intervening to curb population growth and ensure a higher standard of living for more, what would any compassionate being concerned for others and the planet decide? Many spiritual teachers are committed to reminding us of this reality, believing that when people are informed and their loving nature is appealed to, they will embrace the sanity of contraception as a compassionate tool to benefit each and every one of us.

If it is at all possible to avoid what seems to be the inevitable fate of overpopulation, isn't it worth trying to intervene? If we consciously, willfully deploy and encourage the use of contraception, it may be that we can learn to work with the resources we have more wisely.

All this being said, there is a basic premise about contraception that I feel we need to question: what is it that makes contraception work?

There are a number of contraceptive methods. Tantrikas and practitioners of Taoism may use semen retention. This is probably the most advantageous form of contraception as it is least invasive to overall body energy. Tibetan and Indian texts speak of men heating their genitals to kill sperm (at normal temperatures, the testicular sac feels cool) and women washing out their vaginas and stomping their heels firmly on the ground after intercourse. The rhythm method is known throughout the world; there's also widespread understanding of how to work with basal temperature and vaginal viscosity. Those three methods have been used by Catholics for years as a means to circumvent the no-contraception rule, since at least they don't involve artificial objects or chemicals or anything invasive or unnatural. (Even then, the guilt of cheating can put a lid on joy.)

As for devices, chemicals, and other methods created by humans, these have been in existence for centuries. IUD equivalents were used in antiquity not only to block conception physically but to skew the electromagnetic lines of the acupuncture meridians that envelop the uterus; the resulting energetic field was foreign to the fertilized egg, which either couldn't recognize the uterine wall or didn't perceive it to be a viable environment for implantation. Both Ayurvedic and Tibetan medicine, the latter especially being strongly influenced by Buddhist ethics, do include herbal preparations exclusively designed to interfere with or block conception. Their action may be different from that of today's birth control pills and vaginal foams, but the intent is the same. Condoms and well-positioned diaphragms of one form or another are certainly nothing new, even though latex might be. Finally, the modern surgical methods of vasectomies, tubal ligations, and partial or total hysterectomies were very likely known by traditional medical systems, although I am unaware of texts that confirm this.

Any doctor, family planning clinic, or book on birth control can provide statistics on the success level of available modern methods. In any case no method besides total hysterectomy is 100 percent effective. Pregnancies even occur in instances where the man has had a vasectomy or the woman a tubal ligation. Women sometimes get pregnant on the Pill and even more often with diaphragms and condoms—even properly used. Is this a failure on the part of our contraceptive technology? Are people inept or not being truthful about their skill in using these methods? Or is something else going on?

I propose that when conception is meant to happen, nothing will stand in the way. I have met couples well equipped with contraception at conception who have said, "This baby must have really wanted to come." We may be able to alter egg flow or catch sperm, but in the energetic mix of passion, we cannot stop beings who are attached to us from coming into the picture. No matter what wall we throw up to block their becoming, they crawl right over it.

Some people are perfectly successful at blocking conception time and again. Is it possible in some such cases that an entire brood of disembodied consciousnesses lingers around them? And if this seemingly wild notion is so, how would it affect them physically, emotionally, spiritually?

To illustrate this point, the story of a remarkable woman bears telling. When I met her she was pregnant and had one or two other children. She was an artist and a very sensitive woman with deep spiritual values.

Only three or four years earlier, she had been dying of medically diagnosed uterine cancer. A tall, ravishing woman then in her mid-thirties, she had been reduced by the disease to a sixty-pound bedridden shell, barely able to move. While lying there one day, she began to deeply reflect on her predicament. She asked herself the question that probably anyone in her position would ask: "Why is this happening to me?"

In the stillness, a voice came to her. It said, "Because you are afraid to have a child." This truth resonated in her being. She decided to act. Calling her partner, she encouraged him to make love to her—something they had not done in months. She became pregnant, but within a short time she miscarried. Along with the spontaneously aborted fetus, she passed several clots that she reported contained tumors.

Again she asked her partner to make love to her. Again she conceived. Again she miscarried, and with the miscarriage more tumors left her body. Again and again they repeated this act with the same result until, upon medical examination, she was found to be free of all tumors—and pregnant. She soon birthed her first child and went on to have others.

Although this story is extreme, it demonstrates that we have much less control over these matters than we think or than we'd like. There is no certainty that we'll conceive when all is ready: when we've paid off the house, have our finances in order, are between jobs with savings to support us, or have a compelling urge because our biological clock is ticking. Those who cannot conceive—even those with medical diagnoses such as low sperm count to explain their infertility—and those who successfully block conception with contraceptives may simply share the karma of having no being waiting to incarnate that is attracted to them in the first place.

Of course, one can argue that statistics cite low birthrates in populations that do use contraception and high rates in populations that don't. But could it be that the reason for this may have less to do with contraception and more to do with other karmic patterns and tendencies that lead scores of beings to be born in the many dire circumstances available in the world?

Does this mean that we should abandon contraception? No. Such an argument is convincing only up to a certain point. If contraception were merely an illusion, then the great healing traditions of the world would not suggest herbs, observation of a woman's cycle, and so on. They would either teach outright that contraception is a notion of the deluded or they wouldn't address the matter at all.

The most effective contraception probably involves a combination of factors: both partners are equally clear in mind that they are not entertaining the possibility of conceiving; they make this manifest through a birth control method that both feel comfortable and secure with; they skillfully deploy this method during their passion; and there is no being between death and the time for rebirth that is attracted to them.

Still, according to Buddhist thought, we must not to get too smug about this. Anything is possible. If we get caught up in an illusion that leads us to feel we have more control over life than we actually do, then, no doubt, reality will have to knock on our door a little harder than usual. Life is a mystery. What we need and when we need it will naturally arise in the stream of our being. Karma, it bears repeating, is infallible. To want—or not to want—something too rigidly inevitably becomes a source of torment. Especially in the matter of conception, the result of thinking we can control what happens will affect all other areas of intimacy.

> *What we need and when we need it will naturally arise in the stream of our being. Karma is infallible.*

In the path of relationship, the conceiving and raising of children can be the greatest test of our connection to each other within the couple and the extent to which each of us is at one with our own loving nature. Certainly having children is a powerful vehicle for learning what it means to be unconditionally loving and compassionate. We may adamantly want to hold off on such an event in our lives. But if the coming of a child is what we need in order to unfold as "spiritual beings having a human experience," then our efforts to prevent it may be like trying to hold back the tide.

> *Having children is a powerful vehicle for learning what it means to be unconditionally loving and compassionate.*

Thus, as in the amazing story presented earlier, not to conceive year after year may have its own repercussions. To wait or to wait too long while the biological clock ticks on may perhaps be a greater cause for many medical conditions women in modern times are experiencing than our scientific minds are prepared to admit. Repression of our spirit, our emotions, and our biological urges can be costly.

In conclusion, contraception certainly has its place in the natural scheme of things, be it biological or volitional. To my mind we must adopt a Middle Way approach to it—not too loose and not too tight. We can encourage people to have fewer children when they cannot afford them or when they live in an environment that cannot support them. In circumstances where we hold on to a lifestyle of privilege that allows us more freedom of choice, to have to dance to the needs of a small child or two may enrich our personal experience beyond measure and help us to connect with and understand what others in less fortunate circumstances go through.

In these times of change and uncertainty, when we must make so many personal and individual decisions that would have been made for us in the more homogenous cultures and societies of days now past, it stands to reason that parenthood (and even knowing what parenthood should look like) is daunting. Contraception may offer us a "pregnant pause" as we gather our wits to prepare for this awesome role in life. But the intervention may work for a time, forever, or not at all. If we are to remain loving, intimate, and sexual with another, this is the risk we need to accept.

Birth is opportunity and can take many forms. Some of us will best be served by birthing in the flesh. For it is on this level that the true tests of who we are and how effectively we manifest our loving nature will take place.

The Seduction of Infidelity

In *Teachings on Love*, Vietnamese Buddhist master Thich Nhat Hanh speaks of his own culture's understanding of passion and enduring love. The Vietnamese terms *tinh* and *nghia* both mean *love*, but each has a different implication.

Tinh is the heat of passion, the initial lure, the excitement of feeling a connection between you and someone special to you. This kind of love is the most volatile. There can be great inspiration, clarity, and energy with tinh. At the same time, if the mind is untransformed, caught in the Three Poisons of ignorance, attachment, and aggression, then clarity is distorted into fantasy and can be the source of lust and obsession.

Nghia, on the other hand, is the kind of love that builds over time. In the process of meeting opportunities and challenges, the character of love changes and is marked by mutual appreciation and respect.

For a relationship to endure through all of what life offers us, it is nghia, a less passionate but deep love that gradually builds. This does not mean that tinh is no longer there. Rather, there arises a balance that at once keeps the passion of tinh alive in whatever form it may take and establishes the firm, unshakable foundation of nghia. This is what Thich Nhat Hanh calls true love.[1]

In previous chapters I have outlined some challenges our modern-day Western culture presents to enduring love. In the wide-open field of possibilities, the great opportunity for us to meet one another in new, dynamic ways is counteracted with equal force by the possibility of getting lost in too many choices. Without some way of developing discernment, without methods for developing a more awakened state of being in order to connect with our loving nature, it is quite easy to feel ungrounded and lost. And when we feel lost, it is easy to feel disempowered. It is easy to be seduced.

It is the nature of Samsara, the ordinary everyday world untransformed, to be seductive. Without seduction, the Wheel of Samsara would come to a grinding halt. Seduction is the grease that keeps the wheel moving. If it were not for seduction, once we acquired what seduced us in the first place, would we not be satisfied?

Initially we may be, but for how long? For as we immerse ourselves in being with the object of our desire, the thrill of being together begins to dissipate. We then find ourselves repeating all the actions that brought us to who and what we once found delightful as we begin to look elsewhere for satisfaction. The chase itself becomes an integral part of the cycle. The thrill is no longer in having what we want, but in the actual process of getting.

In the end, seduction is nothing more than grasping or attachment inverted. There is nothing out there seducing us. The objects in the world around us are given meaning to us by us. In being seduced we willfully disempower ourselves, allowing ourselves to be carried away by what is, in truth, our own creation. We taunt ourselves with forbidden fruit and by seeking satisfaction through a game of trying to get whatever we cannot consciously ask for directly. In the case of affairs or infatuation with someone new, we may be after something we had with our mate at some point—a connection, a vibrancy, whatever we were seeking or asking for in the beginning—that we have some-how lost. Why do we feel so timid or resigned not to ask our own partner again?

KEEPING BLISS ALIVE

There is the old saying that familiarity breeds contempt. This may be the reason underlying all the other reasons we claim to be the cause for affairs. In *Teachings on Love,* Thich Nhat Hanh gently makes reference to this. Of course, none of us would like to admit that we're in an affair or have had or even considered one out of contempt for our mate. However, if we equate contempt with devaluation, then we can easily see that an affair involves failing to uphold the value of our relationship; it involves valuing something else over the relationship.

Do we lose something permanently in that act of devaluing? When we cross that line and manifest infidelity, is that it? It may be and it may not be. For all situations are ambiguous, and it is how we work with them that defines their meaning and significance. Therefore, in the long run, if a relationship is to survive or not survive an affair, the questions to ask are, What did I learn from this event? and What do I want to do with what I've learned? In the context of Buddhist ethics, these questions are more relevant than the rightness or wrongness of the acts themselves.

For even when speaking of sexual misconduct (which does in-clude infidelity), the Buddha was not prescriptive or dogmatic. He wanted people to contemplate their experience, to develop insight and compassion—not guilt—from what they lived and how they acted.

Let's look at some basic facts. Once we commit to a relationship, we don't then leave our genitals or the hormones that govern them in our partner's purse or coat pocket, or in some drawer in the domicile where we cohabitate. We take them with us wherever we go. We still remain the sexual animals that we are—perhaps more sexually satis-fied sexual animals, committed sexual animals, but sexual animals nonetheless.

To some extent—perhaps less than before but possibly even more—

we continue to be conscious of ourselves in relation to those around us whom we deem attractive. And, no doubt, others still respond to us and even "hit on" us. Some respect our committed relationship. Others want nothing to do with us because we're now out of the running. Still others become all the more attracted to us, either because we show commitment or because we are now the forbidden fruit.

Thus, commitment in a relationship does not end our being a fully functioning hormonal being out in the world, but it does redefine it. We integrate the commitment into our being and it, in turn, modifies our responses to situations and to others. But this does not guarantee that others will necessarily modify their views of and responses to us. People inspire one another with their words, their pecs, their movements, their sunglasses and shiny hair, or the contour of their buttocks highlighted by the satiny shimmer of a skirt. For one reason or another, we will be the object of the attention of others. And we will not be wholly immune from periodically taking a peek at others ourselves.

It would be a nice—a happily ever after—thought to assume that the transformative effects of our relationship would forever modify all of our habitual responses in terms of attraction and love. Initially, this may seem to be the case, but that soon changes. Thich Nhat Hanh brings this reality into focus:

> When you enter a relationship, you feel excitement, enthusiasm, and the willingness to explore. But you may not really understand yourself or the other person very well yet. Living together twenty-four hours a day, you see, hear, and experience many things you have not seen or imagined before. When you fell in love, you constructed a beautiful image that you projected onto your partner, and now you are a little shocked as your illusion disappears and you discover reality. Unless you know how to practice mindfulness together, looking deeply into yourself and your partner, you may find it difficult to sustain your love through this period.[2]

"Unless you know how to practice mindfulness together, looking deeply into yourself and your partner, you may find it difficult to sustain your love."

—THICH NHAT HANH

In time, as the initial allure and energy of passion has been satisfied in the union we have established with our Beloved, we are asked to open a new chapter in how to express our loving nature, moving from the tinh to the nghia aspects of true love. We are on unexplored ground. With the challenge presented by this uncertainty, it is not uncommon for old familiar patterns in our lives to reemerge. We may even think some patterns are gone, but then they begin to raise their horny little heads in the pool of the mundane.

Running alongside our habitual mind and the patterns that have yet to be transformed by our loving nature are the humdrum conditions and circumstances that we hadn't anticipated—or thought only happened to other people. Suddenly we have shared bills and responsibilities. Not so suddenly we have children. Negligees are replaced with T-shirts and sweats or flannel nighties. Late-night parties followed by hours of passion become less frequent or nonexistent, replaced by evenings of balancing the checkbook, trying to get a colicky baby to sleep, and then dropping exhausted into oblivion, dreading to hear the alarm that starts the next day of more of the same. Even when we do squeeze in a night just for us as a couple, the things that used to turn us on seem a bit stale or don't get us there because it's so damn hard to leave the world of concerns that revolves around us wherever we go, even when we lie down and try to let go of it all.

The fact is, what we need from the relationship and from life in general changes over time. In India they speak of the *ashram*s of life, or the stages through which we progress. Each ashram is associated with its life tasks and also highlights the needs we have at any given time at the various levels of our being. Thus, what we need from life and from a relationship at twenty will naturally not be what we need at forty-five. Of course, needs are usually tailgated by wants. And whereas needs tend to be more reality oriented, wants can easily stray into the realm of fantasy.

Habitual mind, circumstance, and the inevitable changes we go through require that we reenvision any long-lasting, loving relationship from time to time. Not to do so is to court disaster. It is to live in an ossified reality resistant to the inevitable. It creates a prison in which either we numb ourselves and reduce our expectations of what life has to offer or we seek release. For some of us, release is sought through affairs. For others, that release may literally occur through death by any number of means, the true source of which is a broken heart—the inability to trust our loving nature sufficiently to know that change is always possible.

> *Habitual mind, circumstance, and the inevitable changes we go through require that we reenvision any long-lasting, loving relationship from time to time.*

So it happens that we go to an aerobics class or we go to work one depressing morning and we notice someone. We talk to this new person, stand close to him or her, and experience a freshness, the scent and sight of something we've somehow lost with our partner. It beckons us, reminding us of what is possible—what we now believe is impossible to feel with the person we live with. We are so tired and bored of living in such a stale situation.

Thus, we reconnect with our own habitual pattern of attraction and connection, not only unencumbered by history but also stimulated by the new needs and wants of the present. It feels new, exhilarating. The heat of passion is alive and stirring within us once more! We reach out and, more than likely, re-create what we had in the beginning with our partner. Maybe it looks different. After all, this is a different person, we've grown, and what we do, need, and want truly has changed. However, the habitual patterns that brought us to this place are probably not that radically different from what got us to the same place with our partner all those months or years ago.

There is a crass American colloquial expression that sums up much of what this situation is about, at least from the standpoint of sexual attraction: "Getting some strange." This expression refers to having a sexual relationship with someone other than the partner you usually have. It implies excitement, risk, even danger. In truth, it harkens back to a naive, adolescent type of infatuation. I suggest here that much of what we feel and what is moving through our minds and bodies in the germinating of affairs is reminiscent of the youthful, hormone-laden, responsibility-free period of our life. The trials and tribulations that are always a part of our history, development, and awakening to our loving nature are obliterated. We bring ourselves to a starting point in something new that has not yet evolved—and may not ever evolve— in any better way or form than what we have created to date. But what the hell!

The power and energy behind these feelings and the new sparks they generate are indeed quite delightful in their own right. It is a pity to see them go out of a relationship, but this usually occurs unintentionally. A myriad of other habitual patterns about how to be in the world surfaces over the course of a lifetime. Having established a relationship and feeling secure in it—at least for the time being—we address other issues in our life, such as money, career, position, and so on. We juggle more and more responsibilities, not seeing how they influence, undermine, and even devalue that initial spark of delight.

The Wheel of Samsara can sometimes feel as if it were slowly grinding us down, and the weight of it all is like a heavy mill wheel. At other times it spins so fast that we can't appreciate anything in the moment; we wish we could just step out of our own lives. With a view not yet wholly transformed, it is only human to reach out for what is light and unencumbered, for someone on whom history has yet to make its mark.

Our loving nature—the source and expression of our enlightenment, our intimate connection to everyone and everything—is about openness, space, and possibility. The ineffable bliss that is an expression of our loving nature unbridled in the experience of full enlightenment reveals itself like a shard of light in moments when our hearts are open. Because of this, we all have a yearning to reach out and immerse ourselves in the bliss that is at once our nature and our birthright. Through the veil of our habitual patterns, we catch a glimpse of it, experiencing for a moment just an ember of that bliss. Then we confuse the bliss with whatever we did to experience it. If we felt that spark in an encounter with someone new, we pursue that person or similar encounters to ensure the same result. This might work for a while. It won't, however, open us up to what is new or to a brighter version of what we glimpsed in the first place. For the bliss we are seeking is far greater than the spark that made us aware of its presence. It is far vaster than we could ever imagine. To merely repeat what we did to experience the spark is to miss the boat altogether. We need to work a little harder, persevere a little longer, reflect a little deeper.

Bliss is not out there. It doesn't arise because of someone else. Its source is our inherent loving nature. Its being is our Buddhanature. Our Beloved, to whom we have opened up, mirrors back to us the glory of ourselves and the love we are willing to open up and share. Living in the truth of this, allowing the spontaneity of this truth to be the ground upon which the two of you meet and grow together, ensures that your Beloved, in turn, also experiences this bliss. It is an experience of both aloneness and togetherness.

For a relationship to serve to bring both partners to such bliss, there are no shortcuts to the exertion that is needed. If we lack this understanding and, further, assume that we know all there is to know about our partner and how far our relationship can take us, the bliss we seek will always elude us.

> *If we assume that we know all there is to know about our partner and how far our relationship can take us, the bliss we seek will always elude us. As soon as we think we know our partner, we have already begun to kill our intimacy.*

Assumptions, in the end, are what deaden a relationship most in the short and long run. As soon as we think we know our partner, we have already begun to kill our intimacy. Like glue, our assumptions bind us to habitual patterns that seemingly get us what we want but, at the same time, gradually leave us stuck in a world of predictable outcomes. Day to day, we look at and respond to our spouse in one particular way and in turn get the same expected response, so that we end up playing the same scenes again and again, like unchanging characters in a bad soap opera. Even if we don't like the scenes, at least they're familiar. We nestle in as under a blanket of seeming security; but, in the end, our security blanket smothers us. Reconnecting with our spouse in fresh, new ways seems a hopeless and hapless task.

In order to feel freshness again, to rekindle what has been lost, escape into the arms of someone new may seem like the only salvation. But in truth, as Pema Chödrön stresses in her writings, there is no escape. We really cannot walk out of our own lives. Wherever we go, there we are. We can indulge in momentary diversions—they may even seem pleasant—but more than likely these just complicate matters and create more mess to clean up now or later on down the road.

Birth, sickness, old age, and death are part of all things that arise in this world. We may have no history, pains, or worries with someone new, but that will all change. History will arise; the pains and worries may be about different things, but they will be there nonetheless.

Not being able to escape our own lives, we need to be willing to fearlessly look at what we do to kill the moment, to deaden ourselves to the experience of aliveness with the ones we love. As stated earlier, we need tools for transforming our Three Poisons of ignorance, attachment, and aggression so that we can come to know our assumptions and expectations and come to understand how they deaden our potentials and do not serve our relationships. Unless we do this work, the turmoil that we now find ourselves in will once again lead to disappointment. It may not give rise to a clandestine affair, but the disappointment will come.

> *To sustain a lasting relationship, we need to fearlessly look at what we do to deaden ourselves to the experience of aliveness with the ones we love.*

As an antidote to wanderlust, I encourage people to visualize in their mind's eye what the affair they are in or are considering might look like in five or ten weeks, months, years. Of course some people want only to have some flings, nothing too serious. These may not involve long-term consequences with another, but they will have far-ranging effects on the primary relationship.

Consider the energy you put into deception. Consider the fact that energetically your spouse does sense what's going on. Try to re-member him or her at the time you first met. Visualize that face, look-ing into those eyes. Now see the uncertainty in your Beloved's eyes and gestures here and now. Visualize looking into those eyes when he or she discovers the deception.

If we choose not to veer down the path of infidelity, how do we handle all those juicy, inspiring feelings that come up with Miss, Madam, or Sir X? We bring the feelings home. We bring them to our partner, to our Beloved.

It helps first to understand that we ourselves have created all those juicy, inspiring feelings. They arise from within us, a relative expres-sion of the bliss of which we are also the source. We fail to see this because we define certain contexts or situations as acceptable, under-standable pathways toward our loving nature. Finding ourselves in those situations, we believe the others who are there to be responsible for the feelings that arise. But they do not give us those feelings. We give ourselves those feelings.

Therefore, if someone does something to turn us on—maybe some-thing we've forgotten about or something new that is the key we need to certain feelings with respect to where we are now—we can note what happens, go home, and create it in our own reality with our Beloved. This might involve new ways of dressing, being, or express-ing ourselves. It might involve experimenting for the first time in a long time. We can honestly tell our partner what we're looking for, what we want from them, whatever is going on inside us. Truth can be an amazing aphrodisiac.

> *Truth can be an amazing aphrodisiac.*

Our partners are usually willing to explore with us ways to re-kindle and invent anew the inspiration that brought us together in the first place. This may seem contrived or unnatural; indeed, our initial efforts may be both. But, in truth, the habitual patterns that we assume are so natural are no less contrived—they are merely familiar. Furthermore, they don't work. So why not try something that shakes up our complacency and takes us out of the dead zone of our comfort?

Of course, we may be able to use old methods we've forgotten about to rekindle bliss. But it's good not to get too nostalgic. For more than likely, because we change over time, what worked in the past may not bring us the bliss we're looking for here and now. As the old Zen saying goes, "You can't step into the same river twice." The water beneath our feet is always new. We need to open up to the present moment. What we had before becomes a building block for what is possible next. It is a foundation, a stepping stone, meant not to hold on to but to step off into new heights and new possibilities.

> *Because we change over time, what worked in the past may not bring us the bliss we're looking for here and now. We need to open up to the present moment.*

DEEPER THOUGHTS ON MONOGAMY

Ultimately, we can learn to love anyone and everyone. In fact, this impartial love is inherent in our loving nature. To quote the great Tibetan physician and Buddhist teacher Gampopa once again, "It is the sign of a superior man that he treat all with equanimity. . . ." When we commit ourselves to one person, it's not as if we'll learn lessons of love—even romantic love—solely from that one person. However, if we can gather up and integrate all that we have learned about love and relationships into a bouquet and offer it to one person, the relationship that is created can be the most powerful vehicle for transformation and growth that we will ever experience.

> *If we can gather up and integrate all that we have learned about love and relationships into a bouquet and offer it to one person, the relationship that is created can be the most powerful vehicle for transformation and growth that we will ever experience.*

It is a rare event when we find such a person in our lives. He or she sings to our heart in a way that transcends culture, race, religion, and the usual things we think about day to day. Perhaps such a mate is as rare as those who connect with dharma, who Buddhist teachers say are as rare as stars in the sky during the day. As there is only one, perhaps one is also the number of mates we can fully, openly embrace at any given time.

To dissipate that energy with other involvements creates a history that goes wide, but not deep. To pursue endless orgasms with another or a host of undemanding beautiful others is like being attracted to the dim lights of the bardo—the in-between state after death and before rebirth. It may satisfy temporarily; it may evoke a glimpse of bliss. But as discussed earlier, bliss evoked in this way is limited by a narrow personal paradigm that clings to what is known. From that place, we can only fear, ignore, or push away a greater bliss, one that has the possibility of running so deep as to have no bounds.

A relationship that endures over time reveals the limitless character, the faceless face of bliss. It embraces Thich Nhat Hanh's principles of tinh and nghia. As we grow in this way individually and as a couple, the power of two loving natures intertwined hastens our own development of wisdom and compassion and spreads out into the world around us, transforming the lives of others. The power of two together creates a synergy far greater than one plus one. What this looks like in concrete terms will vary from one couple to the next and vary over time for each couple. Such couples are chiefly detectable by the loving connection you see when they are together and the warmth experienced by all those around them.

Attraction to others outside of your relationship, whether it manifests as an affair or not, is beckoning you to look more closely at your ignorance, your attachments, and your aggressions, and how they are destroying openness and possibility. For when these Three Poisons are left to flourish without our looking at and transforming them, it is inevitable that assumptions will creep in. Then to keep faith in who we are and in what our relationship means will require such a convoluted effort as to strangle the very life out of us.

We can always transform how we think and act. However, to do so requires faith in the possibility of change. In the wake of wanderlust or an affair, if we are to salvage the relationship, rekindle our deep connection, and move on with our Beloved, we need to embrace and consciously live in the light of our loving nature. Do we have the fortitude to make such a commitment?

Conclusion: An Enduring Love

Ananda said: "Friendship with what is lovely, association with what is lovely, intimacy with what is lovely—that is half of the holy life."

The Buddha responded: "Don't say that, Ananda. It's the whole, not the half of the holy life. One so blessed with what is lovely will develop a right way of being, a thinking that no longer grasps at what is untrue, an aim that is concerned and ready, a contemplation that is unattached and free. Association with what is lovely is the whole of holy life."
—SAMYUTTA NIKAYA, *THE BUDDHA SPEAKS* (P. 41)

As the ceremony of our Buddhist wedding was about to begin, the Venerable Chime Rinpoche took Melanie and me aside. In the quiet of his study he asked us, "Are you a vajra couple?"

Though I knew that *vajra* refers to an unshakable awareness, I am still unsure of what he meant exactly. I believe he was asking, Do we have a bond that has the diamondlike strength and brilliance implied in the term *vajra*? The bottom line was, Are we two made of the kind of stuff that is going to make our marriage a transformative union that endures over time?

When toasts were being made at our reception, I made a speech that reflected this sentiment. I turned to all assembled and put forth the intentions I had in marrying Melanie. Even in the joy of the moment, I was aware that there was work to be done and I was certain that there wasn't anyone I'd rather do it with than my Beloved Melanie. Through it all, this remains as true today as it was then.

What I share in this final chapter are reflections that are a synthesis of what I have come to know from my Buddhist study and practice wedded with the lessons I have learned walking side by side with Melanie. In the long run, a relationship that works is one in which both partners want the relationship to work. As life unfolds and offers the inevitable usual and unusual challenges to their union, both must be solidly grounded in this commitment.

> *In the long run, a relationship that works is one in which both partners want the relationship to work. As life unfolds and offers challenges to their union, both must be solidly grounded in this commitment.*

RECOGNIZING THE RIGHT ONE

We have looked at the Buddha's teaching that over the course of lifetimes we have been mothers, fathers, brothers, sisters, and lovers to countless numbers of beings. This being the case, why should we be surprised that just when we think we have found Mr. or Ms. Right, or even after twenty to twenty-five years of marital and domestic bliss, someone comes along and turns our head—someone we somehow feel connected to? This happens even more easily in these times, when we no longer live in villages where the only boy or girl to meet is the one next door or across the street, or those with whom our parents want us to associate. In the fast pace of modernity, buzzing about more effortlessly in a world less confined by geographic, political, or economic boundaries, we collide into a flurry of karmic connections we have made in countless lifetimes. So much unfinished business.

Considering that this may be the actual situation we find ourselves in, perhaps we are not somehow defective in our abilities to connect and create fruitful loving relationships. Perhaps we are just overwhelmed. Thus, the challenges in meeting our mate are compounded, and the desire and willingness to stay in a committed relationship are rocked as we encounter those with whom our connections may have been intimate and romantic in former times. Then again, it may just be that with the Three Poisons of ignorance, attachment, and aggression untamed, we are set loose in a candy store of possibilities and we just can't help but sample this, taste that.

In either case, we first need to extend kindness and patience to ourselves. Some of us may need to wander through a more complex labyrinth of relationships and trysts in order to gradually piece together the realization and confidence to live in the light of our loving nature. In meeting people with whom we have a connection, we have to decide what that connection means and where we want to go with it this time around. Thus, the longings and affairs some go through and the resulting confusion are no longer viewed as signs of moral corruption, per se, but a process to come to a clear understanding as to what we really want, here and now, in a long-term, loving relationship.

In the long run, the phrase "In sickness and in health" that we used to bind ourselves to another in matrimony or in other conscious partnerships needs to be viewed from a much larger perspective. *Health* we can define as vibrantly living our purpose fueled by the limitless source of our loving nature. *Sickness* refers to succumbing to being caught up in the Three Poisons and how they manifest physically, emotionally, and spiritually. In the realm of duality, sickness and health can be perceived as the light and the shadow. From the nondual perspective of our loving nature, they are of "one taste," each equally valuable as inspiration; we accentuate the light and learn from and transform the darkness that informs us of our disconnection, our alienation. The person before us, our Beloved, is our constant mirror as to where we stand, not only with him or her but, more important, with ourselves.

To embrace the light and the darkness that inevitably come into all relationships is to live in *vajra,* in unshakable awareness. It makes all situations workable. As in the cult film *The Matrix,* it is the "balls to bone" experience the oracle speaks of. If a couple commits—individually and collectively—to working toward a vajra way of life, there is nothing the relationship cannot endure.

WHAT YOU CAN COUNT ON

In a lasting and loving relationship in which both partners are wholly committed to opening fully to their own loving nature, two forces—dharma, the way things are, and drama, the sticky web of entrapment in the Three Poisons—will dance side by side, cheek to cheek, each taking its turn on the dance floor as leader and follower. Consequently, if two people are to survive as a couple, loving each other, it is important that they make friends with contradiction and paradox; that "one taste" can sometimes be as sweet as nectar and, at other times, as foul as dung.

In my twenty-five years of practicing Buddhist ideals in my intimate relationships, I have learned that over the course of time . . .

You will love this person more than anyone else on earth.

You will hate this person more than anyone else on earth.

You will go through times of not feeling anything in particular toward your Beloved.

You will make assumptions about who your Beloved is, and he or she will make assumptions about you.

You won't know who the hell your partner is.

You won't know who the hell you are.

You will do and say things to each other that you'll wish you could go back in time and change.

Your bodies will change.

Your needs will change.

Your wants will change.

You will become intimately familiar with each other's odors, both pleasant and otherwise.

You will have thoughts of others. You will have wanderlust.

You will make a fool of yourself.

You will have regrets.

You will have exquisite memories.

If you make a life together with children, shared concerns, or other shared responsibilities, your loyalties and energies will be split.

You will feel exhausted and spent at times.

There will be gray and black moments, days, perhaps even years.

You will have doubts.

You will feel lonely.

You will feel completed.

You will change and change again.

Your partner will change and change again.

And in the end, one of you will die first.

If you persist, practice patience, open up to the amazing opportunities life with your Beloved offers:

You will grow in unimagined ways.

You will love in unimagined ways.

You will learn to give and receive in unimagined ways.

So long as there is a mutual acknowledgment and respect for the roles each of you plays over the course of the relationship, it doesn't matter who is stronger, weaker, dominant, or subservient. Rest assured, these positions will change anyway. The bottom line is whether or not the relationship you create and persevere in sustains you both and brings you even closer to your essence and reason for being—that is, your loving nature and the overwhelming driving force humans have to love. Residing fearlessly and honestly in your loving nature and gazing into the eyes of your Beloved, you will feel in your heart of hearts the measure of the true value in cultivating enduring love.

To walk hand in hand with your Beloved in the pure radiance of your loving nature is not the only gateway for experiencing a deep and satisfying intimacy with life that the Prince, so long ago, saw as our birthright. But it is by far, at least in the eyes of this seeker, the sweetest of all paths.

Notes

CHAPTER ONE

1. Robert, A. F. Thurman, trans., *The Tibetan Book of the Dead* (New York: Bantam Books, 1994), 46–47.

2. His Holiness the 14th Dalai Lama, *A Policy of Kindness* (Ithaca, N.Y.: Snow Lion Publications, 1990), 109.

3. Lama Ole Nydahl, *The Way Things Are* (Nevada City, Calif.: Blue Dolphin Publishing, 1996), 68.

CHAPTER TWO

1. Lama Ole Nydahl, *The Way Things Are* (Nevada City, Calif.: Blue Dolphin Publishing, 1996), 61–62.

CHAPTER THREE

1. Robert, A. F. Thurman, trans., *The Tibetan Book of the Dead* (New York: Bantam Books, 1994), 244.

CHAPTER FIVE

1. Sengstan, *Hsin Hsin Ming: Sengstan's Verses on the Faith-Mind* (Fredonia, N.Y.: White Pine Press, 1984).

2. Rainer Maria Rilke, *Rilke on Love and Other Difficulties*, trans. John J. L. Mood (New York: Norton, 1975), 27, 28.

CHAPTER SIX

1. Tenzin Wangyal Rinpoche, *The Tibetan Yogas of Dream and Sleep* (Ithaca, N.Y.: Snow Lion Publications, 1998), 215.

2. Sogyal Rinpoche, *The Tibetan Book of Living and Dying* (San Francisco: HarperSanFrancisco, 1994), 92.

3. Dharmarakshita, *The Wheel of Sharp Weapons* (Dharamsala, India: Library of Tibetan Works and Archives, 1981), verse 25.

4. Ibid., verse 23.

5. Ibid., verse 15.

6. Ibid., verse 21.

7. Ibid., verse 18.

8. Jamgon Kongtrul, *The Great Path of Awakening* (Boston: Shambhala Publications, 1996), 32.

CHAPTER SEVEN

1. Gedun Chöpel, "The Treatise on Passion" in *Tibetan Arts of Love* (Ithica, N.Y.: Snow Lion Publications, 1992), 92.

CHAPTER EIGHT

1. Gedun Chöpel, "The Treatise on Passion" in *Tibetan Arts of Love* (Ithaca, N.Y.: Snow Lion Publications, 1992), 144.

2. Terry Clifford, *Tibetan Buddhist Medicine and Psychiatry* (York Beach, Maine: Samuel Weiser, 1984), 219.

3. Robert Sachs, *Tibetan Ayurveda* (Rochester, Vt.: Healing Arts Press, 2001), 128.

4. Gedun Chöpel, *Tibetan Arts of Love*, 144.

5. Ibid, 144.

6. Nik Douglas and Penny Slinger, *Sexual Secrets: The Alchemy of Ecstasy* (Rochester, Vt.: Destiny Books, 2000), 282.

7. Kalu Rinpoche, *The Gem Ornament of Manifold Oral Instructions* (San Francisco: KDK Publications, 1986), 99.

8. Gedun Chöpel, *Tibetan Arts of Love*, 160.

9. Robert Sachs, *Tibetan Ayurveda*, 140.

CHAPTER NINE

1. Andrew Cohen, *Embracing Heaven and Earth* (Lenox, Mass.: Moksha Press, 2000), 89–93.

CHAPTER ELEVEN

1. Thich Nhat Hanh, *Teachings on Love* (Berkeley: Parallax Press, 1998), 65.

2. Ibid., 86.

Bibliography

Bancroft, Anne, ed. *The Buddha Speaks*. Boston: Shambhala Publications, 2000.

Bartok, Josh, ed. *Daily Wisdom: 365 Buddhist Inspirations*. Somerville, Mass.: Wisdom Publications, 2001.

Chödrön, Pema. *The Wisdom of No Escape*. Boston: Shambhala Publications, 2001.

Chöpel, Gedun. *Tibetan Arts of Love*. Ithaca, N.Y.: Snow Lion Publications, 1992.

Clifford, Terry. *Tibetan Buddhist Medicine and Psychiatry*. York Beach, Maine: Samuel Weiser, 1984.

Cohen, Andrew. *Embracing Heaven and Earth*. Lenox, Mass.: Moksha Press, 2000.

Dalai Lama, His Holiness the 14th. *A Policy of Kindness*. Ithaca, N.Y.: Snow Lion Publications, 1990.

———. *The Dalai Lama's Book of Daily Meditations*. London: Rider Press, 1998.

Dharmarakshita. *The Wheel of Sharp Weapons*. Dharamsala, India: Library of Tibetan Works and Archives, 1981.

Dorje, Chekawa Yeshe. *The Seven Points of Mind Training*. Revised edition. Dharamsala, India: Library of Tibetan Works and Archives, 1981.

Douglas, Nik, and Penny Slinger. *Sexual Secrets: The Alchemy of Ecstasy*. Rochester, Vt.: Destiny Books, 2000.

Ellenberg, Dr. Daniel, and Judith Bell. *Lovers for Life*. Santa Rosa, Calif.: Aslan Publishing, 1995.

Evans-Wentz, W. Y. *Tibetan Yoga and Secret Doctrines*. Oxford: Oxford University Press, 2000.

Kalu Rinpoche. *The Gem Ornament of Manifold Oral Instructions*. San Francisco: KDK Publications, 1986.

Karthar Rinpoche, Khenpo. *Dharma Paths*. Ithaca, N.Y.: Snow Lion Publications, 1992.

———. *The Instructions of Gampopa*. Ithaca, N.Y.: Snow Lion Publications, 1996.

Kongtrul, Jamgon. *The Great Path of Awakening*. Boston: Shambhala Publications, 1996.

Nydahl, Lama Ole. *Entering the Diamond Way*. Nevada City, Calif.: Blue Dolphin Publishing, 1990.

———. *The Way Things Are*. Nevada City, Calif.: Blue Dolphin Publishing, 1996.

Sachs, Robert. *Tibetan Ayurveda*. Rochester, Vt.: Healing Arts Press, 2001.

Schumann, H. W. *The Historical Buddha*. London: Arkana, 1990.

Sengstan. *Hsin Hsin Ming: Sengstan's Verses on the Faith-Mind*. Fredonia, N.Y.: White Pine Press, 1984.

Seung Sahn, the Venerable. *Dropping Ashes on the Buddha*. New York: Grove Press, 1994.

Sogyal Rinpoche. *The Tibetan Book of Living and Dying*. San Francisco: HarperSanFrancisco, 1994.

Thich Nhat Hanh. *Present Moment, Wonderful Moment*. Berkeley: Parallax Press, 1990.

———. *Teachings on Love*. Berkeley: Parallax Press, 1998.

Thurman, Robert A. F., trans. *The Tibetan Book of the Dead*. New York: Bantam Books, 1994.

Trungpa, Chögyam. *Cutting Through Spiritual Materialism*. Boston: Shambhala Publications, 1987.

Wangyal Rinpoche, Tenzin. *The Tibetan Yogas of Dream and Sleep*. Ithaca, N.Y.: Snow Lion Publications, 1998.

About the Author

In his desire to be of practical service in the various life stages of others, Robert's education and training has been an eclectic blend of both ancient and contemporary healing and wisdom traditions. He began to study with Buddhist masters in Scotland while attending the University of Lancaster in England in the early 1970s. Inspired to pursue the practice of hatha yoga and meditation, after he received his Bachelor of Arts in Comparative Religion and Sociology, he went to London to train both as a mental health counselor and to engage in a rigorous study of yogic disciplines and oriental healing. In 1976 he became certified as a hatha yoga instructor with the All India Board and Inner London Education Authority. He completed shiatsu training with shiatsu master Rex Lassalle in 1978 and was instrumental in starting the Community Health Foundation's Growing Family Center.

When Robert returned to the United States with his wife, Melanie, his knowledge of healing and the role of spirit were deepened with the sudden infant death of their daughter Shamara in 1981. This prompted Robert to do further training and receive his Masters in Social Work at the University of Kentucky and, at the same time, to begin the study of conscious dying practices as found in the Tibetan Buddhist tradition. Trained in the Tibetan practice of phowa or transference of consciousness at the moment of death by phowa master Lama Ole Nydahl, Robert went on to become a hospice social worker and a member of Sogyal Rinpoche's Spiritual Dying Network in 1995. He wrote two books on death and dying: *Rebirth Into Pure Land*, the remarkable story of the death of his daughter Shamara, and in 1998, *Perfect Endings: A Conscious Approach to Death and Dying*.

Robert's interest in the area relationships prompted him to work with a number of social work and psychotherapeutic models; study oriental astrology (especially in the field of what today is called Feng Shui Astrology or Nine Star Ki—in which he is considered one of the foremost western authorities); and study under numerous Buddhist masters, including the Venerable Chime Rinpoche, Khenpo Karthar Rinpoche, Kalu Rinpoche, Venerable Chögyam Trungpa Rinpoche, Lama Ole Nydahl, Zen master Seung Sahn, and his primary teacher, His Holiness Kunzig Shamar Rinpoche.

Robert works nationally and internationally with physicians, clinics, hospitals, private individuals, meditation groups, community-based organizations, and private corporations, teaching them how to integrate contemporary scientific approaches with the ancient wisdom traditions in the areas of stress management, preventive health care, and interpersonal and transpersonal communication. Robert has also appeared on and hosted his own radio shows, both in the United States and Europe. In addition to his two books on dying, he is also the author of *Tibetan Ayurveda: Health Secrets from the Roof of the World* (originally published in 1995 as *Health for Life*) and *Nine-Star Ki: Your Astrological Companion to Feng Shui.*

Robert met has wife, Melanie, in England in 1975 and they married in the late summer of 1976. Together they direct Diamond Way Ayurveda, which provides products and educational services to the spa, massage, and beauty industries in the preventive health care and Ayurvedic bodywork methods of India and Tibet. They have three children: Kai Ling, Harriet Christina, and Jabeth David-Francis.

For further information, the author may be contacted at the following address:

Robert Sachs
P.O. Box 13753
San Luis Obispo, CA 93406
805-543-9291 (phone and fax)
passionate8@earthlink.net
Websites:
  www.DiamondWayAyurveda.com
  www.NineStarKi.net

Index

Books of Related Interest

A Sacred Sex Devotional
365 Inspiring Thoughts to Enhance Intimacy
Edited by Rafael Lorenzo

Eros, Consciousness, and Kudalini
Deepening Sensuality through Tantric Celibacy and Spiritual Intimacy
by Stuart Sovatsky, Ph.D.

Breathing
Expanding Your Power and Energy
by Michael Sky

Mastery of Awareness
Living the Agreements
by Doña Bernadette Vigil with Arlene Broska, Ph.D.

Earthwalks for Body and Spirit
Exercises to Restore Our Sacred Bond with the Earth
by James Endredy

Taming the Tiger
Tibetan Teachings on Right Conduct, Mindfulness, and Universal Compassion
by Akong Tulku Rinpoche

Zen and the Psychology of Transformation
The Supreme Doctrine
by Hubert Benoit

Tantric Awakening
A Woman's Initiation into the Path of Ecstasy
by Valerie Brooks

Inner Traditions • Bear & Company
P.O. Box 388
Rochester, VT 05767
1-800-246-8648
www.InnerTraditions.com

Or contact your local bookseller